CARL BERGER is a member of the Department of History at the University of Toronto.

Professor Berger aims in this book to 'explore the rise, expression, and relative decline of the idea of natural history' in Canada during the age of Victoria. Science, particularly natural science, was then accessible to the general public in a way scarcely imaginable today. Natural history societies were set up in a number of cities and provided a focus for the descriptive and collecting activities of amateurs and incipient professionals. These societies acted as social clubs and vehicles for self-improvement as well as providing excellent training for the amateur scientist. The Baconian assumptions that inspired the Victorian collectors and scientists were one of the major victims of the Darwinian revolution, and their demise brought about the gradual decline of the natural history societies.

Professor Berger considers also the sense of wonder and reverence with which Victorian Canadians, like their British contemporaries, looked at the varieties and delights of nature. The British tradition of natural theology had a great impact on the pursuit of science in Victorian Canada, leading naturalists and poets alike to seek in the uncharted flora and fauna of their new land the handiwork of a benevolent God. The author examines the impact of the discoveries of Darwin on this tradition and on the relations between science and religion, as the creator and the act of creation became more and more distant in time and more tenuously connected to the world of nature around us.

His study provides many rich insights into the practice and theory of natural history in an age when even a veteran politician could look back and recall, with understanding and in detail, the world of nature in the countryside of his youth.

THE JOANNE GOODMAN LECTURES

Delivered at the University of Western Ontario

SCIENCE, GOD, AND NATURE IN VICTORIAN CANADA

The 1982 Joanne Goodman Lectures
CARL BERGER

University of Toronto Press
Toronto Buffalo London

© University of Toronto Press 1983
Toronto Buffalo London
Printed in Canada

ISBN 0-8020-2501-3 (cloth)
ISBN 0-8020-6523-6 (paper)

Canadian Cataloguing in Publication Data

Berger, Carl, 1939–
  Science, God, and nature in Victorian Canada

  (The Joanne Goodman lectures ; 1982)
  Includes bibliographical references and index.
  ISBN 0-8020-2501-3 (bound). – ISBN 0-8020-6523-6 (pbk.)

  1. Natural history – Canada – History – 19th century –
  Addresses, essays, lectures. I. Title. II. Series:
  The Joanne Goodman memorial lectures ; 1982.

  QH21.C3B47   508.71   C83-098295-7

The Joanne Goodman Lecture Series

has been established by Joanne's family

and friends to perpetuate the memory of her

blithe spirit, her quest for knowledge, and

the rewarding years she spent at the

University of Western Ontario.

The Natural History of our country is worthy of study on account of the great importance of many natural objects and processes to our subsistence and comfort; on account of the interest and beauty connected with nearly everything in nature; and on account of the evidence which it affords of the power, wisdom, and goodness of the Creator.

John William Dawson *A Hand Book of the Geography and Natural History of the Province of Nova Scotia for the Use of Schools, Families, and Travellers* 4th edition, revised (Pictou 1857)

Contents

Picture credits

The illustrations appear following page xiv.

Three Canadian plants: *Canadian Wild Flowers, Painted and Lithographed by Agnes Fitzgibbon with Botanical Description by C.P. Traill* (Montreal 1868) 28

Sir Daniel Wilson: *Dominion Illustrated* 22 March 1890

John Macoun: *The Autobiography of John Macoun* (Ottawa 1922)

James Fletcher: Public Archives of Canada / PA 130492

A naturalist's notebook: Public Archives of Prince Edward Island, Accession #2353, Francis Bain Papers

Abbé Léon Provancher: Victor-Alphonse Huard *La Vie et l'oeuvre de l'abbé Provancher* (Quebec 1926)

Sir William Dawson: McGill University Archives

Foreword

The Joanne Goodman Lectures at the University of Western Ontario were established in 1975 to honour the memory of the elder daughter of Mr and Mrs Edwin A. Goodman of Toronto. The general theme of the series is the history of the English-speaking peoples, with particular attention being devoted to the countries of the Atlantic Triangle – Canada, the United Kingdom, and the United States. Each year the university invites a distinguished scholar to deliver three public lectures to an audience of students, faculty, and members of the general community. The list at the front of this volume of those who have so far participated in the series is an indication of the distinction of the lectures and of the important part they play in the intellectual life of the institution. The University of Western Ontario is grateful to Mr and Mrs Goodman and their family and friends for this generous and moving benefaction dedicated to a student who loved history and enjoyed her years at Western.

Professor Carl Berger of the Department of History, University of Toronto, is well known to students of Canadian history as one of the country's leading intellectual historians. His studies of Canadian imperialists before the First World War, *The Sense of Power* (1970), and of English-Canadian historians, *The Writing of Canadian History* (1976), are acknowledged masterpieces; for the latter he received the Governor General's Award. Professor

Berger brings the same qualities of lucidity, brevity, and literary grace to his third major subject, natural history in Victorian Canada. He demonstrates that this was no technical specialty but a popular activity in which a wide variety of educated people participated and made contributions. He shows how the adaptations of European scientific discoveries fit into and illuminate a colonial pattern and elaborates W.L. Morton's observation that the most substantial intellectual achievement of Victorian Canada was in science. Canada was part of the international scientific community in the nineteenth century, and in Sir William Dawson it had the leading anti-Darwinian in the English-speaking world. But above all, Professor Berger reminds us of the protean interests, the indefatigable energy, and the determination of the Victorians who came, saw, and catalogued the frontiers of the Western world and in so many ways shaped this country. We at the University of Western Ontario were fortunate to be the first to hear these stimulating lectures, and we are pleased that the terms of the lecture trust assist in making them available to that wider audience that they so richly deserve.

Neville Thompson
The University of Western Ontario

Preface

The nineteenth century witnessed an astonishing extension and diversification of science, and natural history was in the forefront of this development. In the mid-Victorian years natural history denoted an encyclopaedic study of all objects in nature, and it incorporated approaches that would in time become compartmentalized into botany and zoology, ethnology and meteorology. Though geology, the queen of the sciences, early established a specialized status, it was often incorporated within the vague boundaries of natural history. The Victorian reader who took up a work in popular natural history on a particular area, or a periodical published by a natural history society, expected to find descriptions of animals, birds, and fish, as well as geological structures; a record of natural events during the seasons of the year; some evocation of the scenery; and even discussions of backwoodsmen and settlement and accounts of the societies and legends of the native peoples. The primary mission of natural history was to collect, describe, and classify the flora and fauna, and identify and trace the geological formations, of new, unknown territories. This purpose was well within the mainstream of British and American natural science at least until the 1860s, and in Canada it was promoted at many levels – by gifted individuals; by the government agencies, especially the Geological Survey; and by local societies. Natural history was an accessible form of science: in Victorian Canada it enjoyed a popular existence, and its history must find room not only for such outstanding individuals of international reputation as the geologist Sir John William Dawson, but also for more humble naturalists whose activities attested to the assumption that a familiarity with natural history was part of the mental equipment of every educated person.

If we are to understand the reasons why this awareness of nature bulked larger in the imaginations of Victorians than it was ever to do again, we must rid our minds of two anachronisms. Science then was not remote, forbidding, and abstruse. Like Canada itself the life sciences were in their infancy or adolescence and their mission and methods could with some application be readily comprehended by the educated layman. The pursuit of natural history, moreover, has somehow come to be associated with the quaint, frivolous, and eccentric. In some uninformed quarters it then had the same connotations: when the villagers at Percé noticed the geologist Sir William Logan tracing formations, pacing off measured steps and counting to himself aloud, striking stones with his hammer and wrapping some in paper and depositing them in a bag, they pitied him as a lunatic or idiot and two men seized him with the intention of putting him on the first boat to Beauport, the nearest asylum. Such anecdotes became part of the lore of natural history and gave the subject a faint aura of oddity. But to the educated in Victorian times it was a fashionable and respectable pursuit. It could be mere collecting, an occasional amusement, and an inconsequential diversion. But it was possible for observant naturalists by avocation to bring to light new facts that were important to science.

One of the most distinctive features of natural history was the association of the study of nature with aesthetic appreciation and religious feelings. The support for science in a colonial society was no doubt heavily utilitarian, but natural history also impinged on the minds of thoughtful Victorians because for them nature was the handiwork of God and its patterns and operations disclosed His wisdom, power, and goodness. They were, in addition, compelled to come to terms with two revolutionary visions of nature. The first came from geology, which informed them that the earth had not always been what they saw around them, but that it was a museum containing the archives of an inconceivably ancient history of stupendous and sometimes violent changes. The second was Charles Darwin's theory of evolution through natural selection. These discoveries carried disturbing implications within science itself, and for the literate public they bore directly upon traditional and scriptural explanation of man's place in creation. This too intensified an interest in natural history beyond the confines of scientific circles.

The history of this branch of knowledge in Canada is not the story of the development of totally original ideas, nor is it the record of sensational discoveries. Historians of science long ago abandoned the study of the past as a chronicle of progress leading from one major breakthrough to another and have increasingly concentrated upon science as a social activity and upon the interplay between its practice, its claims, and its developing institutions and the matrix in which these take place. This is an altogether more appropriate approach to colonial natural history. The late W.L. Morton, who once wrote that the most substantial intellectual achievement of Victorian Canada was in science, and not literature or theology, put the matter exactly when he said that science in such a setting is more a matter of reproducing and consolidating institutions and ways of thinking than of altering and renovating.[1] The implanting and growth of science in Victorian Canada was one strand in a complex fabric of transplanted British civilization overseas; like other strands in that culture it was modified and the resulting pattern was not an exact duplication. Nor was it entirely a matter of borrowing. Canadian naturalists belonged to an international community, and their contributions to science were recognized abroad long before it was ever admitted that the country had a history, still less a literature.

These lectures then set out to explore the rise, expression, and relative decline of the idea of natural history. The first lecture will deal with the emergence of scientific institutions, especially the natural history societies which were among the earliest organizations of Canadian intellectual activity. The second will attempt to convey something of that sense of wonder and reverence evoked by natural history for Victorians and will consider the ways in which religion pervaded its procedures and practices. The third will examine the reception of Darwin's theory of evolution among Canadian naturalists. My purpose is not to trace the internal history of any particular branch of science, but rather to suggest the range and vitality of Victorian natural history, explain some of the reasons for its popularity in a colonial culture, and thereby bring its history into somewhat closer touch with the more familiar aspects of the nineteenth-century past.

I am grateful to Suzanne and Edwin Goodman for the opportunity to give these lectures and President George Connell and Professor Neville Thompson of the University of Western Ontario and their colleagues for their attention and hospitality. Among the many who have aided me with the research and must be thanked – regretfully anonymously – are the archivists and librarians at the Public Archives of Canada, the National Library, the National Museums of Canada, the McGill University Archives, the Public Archives of Nova Scotia, the libraries of the University of Toronto, and the Royal Ontario Museum. Glenn Wright of the Public Archives went far beyond all reasonable calls of duty in locating some of the illustrations. Ramsay Cook, Bert Hansen, and Trevor Levere gave me the benefit of their thoughtful and constructive comments on an earlier version of the text. And I owe a very special debt to the late Sam Waller, companion and collector-naturalist of the old school, who introduced me to the world of natural history and would have been amused by one of the results.

Three Canadian plants – yellow adders tongue, trillium, and
columbine – painted by Agnes Fitzgibbon, 1868

Sir Daniel Wilson

John Macoun

James Fletcher addressing an excursion of the botanical section of the Ottawa Field Naturalists' Club at MacKay's Grove, May 1901

A naturalist's notebook: detail of a page from the journal of Francis Bain, July 1877

Abbé Léon Provancher

Sir William Dawson

1 ～

Science

NATURAL HISTORY WAS born of wonder and nurtured by greed, and it combined an intellectual fascination with the strange forms of life in northern America with an intense interest in exploiting new resources. These twin motives lay back of the earliest notices of plants, animals, and minerals that were recorded by the first explorers, missionaries, royal officials, Hudson's Bay Company officers, and plant-hunters, usually professional gardeners, who searched out exotic species to adorn the greenhouses of their aristocratic patrons.

These forays were initiated from metropolitan centres, and for a long time Canada remained in science what she was in economics – a collecting ground and an exporter of raw material. The beginnings of a science conducted by indigenous naturalists were tentatively laid early in the nineteenth century by immigrants who brought to the colonies a popular British tradition that combined an appreciation for the utility of scientific knowledge with a gentle, almost reverential attitude to the natural world. These beginnings, however, were unprepossessing and fragile. In the thin and anaemic cultural fabric of the colonies the status of science was measured in modest ways – in the number of microscopes possessed by individuals or institutions, or by collections brought together by amateurs such as Thomas McCulloch, the founder of the Pictou Academy, whose cabinet of birds surprised and impressed John James Audubon. The personal histories of even the most determined of these isolated naturalists were often chronicles of disappointment and frustration. Charles Fothergill, a Yorkshire Quaker who arrived in Upper Canada in 1816 with the impossible dream of compiling an inventory of nature of the whole Empire, possessed an insatiable curiosity about everything in the new landscape of ugly stumps, about the citizens, especially the Yankees whose manners he abhorred and whose coarse features he attributed to excessive meat eating, and about the three Indian women whom he chased about a deserted house in Kingston and who emitted sounds that he compared – true naturalist that he was – to the cries of young turkeys.[1] In spite of his extensive involvement in the political and journalistic life of the colony Fothergill managed to put on record the first extensive descriptions of its birds, mammals, and reptiles and to paint many of them; but after his death in 1840 most of his specimens were destroyed in a fire, and his invaluable manuscript notes and illustrations were lost for almost a century.

Another extraordinary naturalist, Andrew Downs of Halifax, partially succeeded where Fothergill had failed and created the first zoological garden in British North America. Possibly inspired by his acquaintance with Charles Waterton, an Englishman renowned for his eccentricity of behaviour and the founder of the first bird sanctuary, at Walton Hall, Yorkshire, Downs started his zoo in 1847 on a few acres at the head of the North West Arm. In time his gothic cottage, filled with case upon case of specimens of every description, a herbarium, and many paintings, and surrounded by a horticultural garden and grounds containing an astonishing menagerie of monkeys, bears, deer, moose, beavers, and birds from all over the world, became a source of pleasure and instruction to visitors to Halifax. An authority on birdlife and an expert taxidermist, Downs supplied specimens to many museums in America and Europe (including the personal collection of King Victor Emmanuel of Italy).[2]

The efforts of these and other individuals were paralleled by the emergence of organized circles of naturalists in Quebec and Montreal in the 1820s. Though the Literary and Historical Society of Quebec, initiated by Lord Dalhousie in 1824, was intended primarily to preserve historical records, a substantial proportion of the addresses thought worthy of publication in its transactions were of a scientific character, including reports on the geology of the Great Lakes, notes on plants, an account of the northern lights, and descriptions of the coral animals of the St Lawrence. The Quebec society and the Natural History Society of Montreal, which was founded in 1827 and supported by members of the Anglo-Scottish commercial élite, medical doctors, ministers, and teachers from McGill College, concentrated upon the indispensable preliminaries – buying books to build scientific libraries, acquiring instruments for mineralogical observations, and assembling cabinets of geological and botanical specimens. The group in Montreal seemed on the whole more intent on popularizing natural science than in original research, and most of the papers read at meetings were either straightforward accounts of resources or on such general, assigned topics as the origins of differences in the human races or the causes of earthquakes and volcanoes. Even these modest aspirations, however, seemed premature. By the 1840s both societies were moribund – the one at Quebec a victim of the ethnic conflicts of the 1837 rebellion and the transfer of the capital to Kingston, the one in Montreal a casualty of the unsettling effects of the commercial realignments.[3] The successor of the Montreal society was to claim among its achievements support for the creation of the Geological Survey of Canada in 1842. But the Geological Survey, which was charged with searching for economic minerals and was to become the most important scientific institution in Victorian Canada, led an uncertain existence in the 1840s and 1850s.

It was only in the 1850s, a decade that witnessed the consolidation of so many tendencies in British North American life, that these scattered and tentative beginnings matured with the appearance of self-sustaining societies devoted to natural science. Between 1849, when the Canadian Institute was set up in Toronto, and 1890, when the Natural History Society of British Columbia was organized in Victoria, Canadians created a number of local scientific institutions that were remarkable for the scope of their activities and relative popularity. The most important of these centres – the revitalized Natural History Society of Montreal, the Nova Scotia Institute of Natural Science (1862), the Hamilton Association for the Cultivation of Literature, Science and Art (1857), the Natural History Society of New Brunswick (1863), the Natural History Society of Ottawa (1863), which became the

Ottawa Field Naturalists' Club in 1879, and the Manitoba Historical and Scientific Society (1879) – all at one time or another published substantial transactions that brought the results of Canadian efforts in natural history to the attention of an international scientific community.

The organization and maintenance of these societies represented a growing appreciation on the part of the public – at least as this was indicated by the decisions of politicians – of the economic value of science in locating ore bodies, controlling insect infestations, maintaining accurate meteorological records that would permit prediction of weather patterns, assessing the suitability of new lands for agricultural settlement, and advertising Canadian resources at international expositions. Economic entomology, for example, assumed an important place because of the spectacular outbreaks of insects destructive to crops and the rapid spread of species introduced from Europe. The Entomological Society of Canada, which had been organized in 1863 by Charles Bethune, an Anglican priest and later master of Trinity College School at Port Hope, and William Saunders, a London pharmacist and fruit-grower, had initially confined itself to linking collectors in various parts of Canada and in compiling lists. Requested by the Ontario government to submit advice on checking the damage done by the Colorado beetle, Bethune and Saunders turned more directly to insect control and received continuing support for their journal, the *Canadian Entomologist*, on condition that they submit annual reports to the minister of agriculture. Similar, though not identical, considerations led to the creation of the Experimental Farm in Ottawa in 1886 and the hiring of a Dominion Entomologist. This official acknowledgment of the economic usefulness of science provided a major incentive and justification for the natural history societies (most major ones received direct financial aid from the provinces to publish their periodicals) and enabled them in turn to argue that the diffusion of such useful knowledge would almost automatically lead to economic growth.

The status of the natural sciences was further enhanced in the middle decades of the century by the establishment of chairs of natural history in the colleges and the inclusion of scientific subjects in programs of study. Many of those appointed to these posts had themselves received some elements of formal training in Scotland. James Robb, who began instructing in natural history and chemistry at King's College, Fredericton, in 1837, held a medical degree from Edinburgh and had attended lectures in science in Paris; the Nova Scotia–born geologist William Dawson, the principal of McGill after 1855, had also taken courses at Edinburgh; and George Lawson had studied and tutored in botany there for a decade before arriving at Queen's University, Kingston, in 1858. This strong connection with the 'Athens of the North,' which was far in advance of the two old English universities in most scientific matters, was complemented by a variety of other academic traditions and levels of training. At University College, Toronto, the chair of natural history was held by the Reverend William Hincks, a former Presbyterian clergyman turned Unitarian, who had taught at Queen's College, Cork; two of his colleagues, the chemist Henry Croft and the geologist Edward Chapman, were Englishmen with degrees from German universities. Loring Woart Bailey succeeded Robb at Fredericton in 1861 fresh from the scientific vitality of the Harvard of Louis Agassiz and Asa Gray.

Whatever their backgrounds, this first generation of academic scientists – the word itself only became current after 1840 – shared certain experiences and attitudes. Since science instruction consisted for the most part in imparting an understanding of general, elementary principles, and since the boundaries between the sciences were porous, natural history was initially taught in conjunction with nearly all the other sciences by a single individual. Though specialized fields were recognized early at Toronto and McGill, in smaller centres the tradition of the omniscience persisted. For nearly half a century Bailey at Fredericton was responsible for physics, chemistry, zoology, physiology, botany, and geology. These teachers came in at the beginning: in order to familiarize students with their own natural surroundings they began the collection of natural history material and wrote manuals and texts. Most of them became men with a mission, of advancing an appreciation of scientific culture both within the academies and among the general public. Together with men from the Geological Survey they were leaders in founding and sustaining the local scientific societies and in giving editorial direction to their publications. While at Queen's, Lawson established the Botanical Society of Canada to carry out a systematic stock-taking of the country's plant resources; later, at Dalhousie, he supported the local society and for years worked for the provincial board of agriculture. Dawson almost single-handedly resuscitated the failing Natural History Society of Montreal and helped make its journal, the *Canadian Naturalist and Geologist*, a pre-eminent publication. The *Canadian Journal of Industry, Science and Art*, put out by the Canadian Institute in Toronto, was originally restricted to the professional concerns of engineers, architects, and surveyors; but under the editorship of Hincks and later of Daniel Wilson, a professor of English and history whose real love was ethnology, it became a more catholic periodical, in which natural history figured prominently. These and other academic scientists took as their models the heroes of science of Victorian Britain who were zealous promoters and who addressed popular audiences, mechanics' institutes, and even school children no less frequently than they communicated discoveries to their fellow scientists.

To this increasing recognition of the utility of science and the guiding role of naturalists in universities and government must be added two other, more elusive, factors that favoured the emergence and maintenance of societies. Though science was regarded as essentially cosmopolitan, a sense of colonial self-awareness and a striving for a measure of self-reliance entered into at least the justifications for a more intense devotion to natural history. Throughout the century the colonies and the new

Dominion incurred huge deficits in terms of the intellectual balance of trade, borrowing much and sending back little in return. Given the relative simplicity and accessibility of natural history, and the alluring opportunities presented by an area scarcely described in depth, the practice of this science was one way for Canadians to add to the stock of knowledge and assert a certain intellectual status.

In Victorian Britain natural history was both a disciplined, scientific quest and a fashionable diversion that touched all layers of society and was manifested in many ways – in the aquarium, fern case, and shell collection displayed in the drawing-room; participation in evenings devoted to viewing the wonders of nature through the microscope; outings into the countryside armed with plant box or geologist's hammer; and visits to zoological gardens, once the exclusive preserves of the wealthy, but now public institutions for the multitudes. This curiosity was no less evident in the proliferation of literature on the romance of natural history, the appearance of lavishly illustrated guides to the flowering plants of individual counties, and the popularity of travel books, which always contained descriptions of nature in strange places. The Victorians took for granted that a familiarity with natural science and a sensitivity to scenery formed part of the intellectual equipment of every educated person. Those English travellers who wrote accounts of the societies of the colonial settlements invariably assumed that their readers would be interested not only in natural wonders – the ice cone at Montmorency or the falls at Niagara – but also in their descriptions of the New World's animals, birds, and plants. The fad of natural history was most evident in the fashion for making one's own collection of natural history objects. The materials were accessible and the equipment minimal, and everything had a place within the orderly Linnaean system of classification in which each item was described by two names – one referring to the family, the other to the particular species. A system of classification was not in itself an incentive to study nature, but it did provide a necessary framework for collecting and, by holding out the prospect that even a dilletante could discover something new, for popular participation in science. Natural history in Victorian culture was associated with wealth and religion and with self- and social improvement and was sanctioned as a 'rational amusement.'[4]

The natural history societies of colonial Canada were dedicated to the perpetuation and extension of this British tradition of popular science no less than to advancing the claims of science as applied to agriculture, commerce, and industry. Though they do not have one common history, they shared a consensus on purposes and procedures.[5] Bound by their constitutions to hold regular meetings for discussion, maintain libraries of useful books and periodicals as well as museums, and to sponsor public lectures, they attracted members whose attainments varied and whose interests ranged from tepid curiosity to intense application. Several of these groups came together by the influence of strongly motivated and inspirational individuals – the enthusiasts who served as officers, edited the transactions, wrote a large proportion of the papers, and led the summer field excursions. When the secretary of the Nova Scotian Institute noted in 1895 that only a quarter of the 126 members had ever published reports he isolated an experience common to all societies. (In 1885 the Montreal society claimed 287 members; the Nova Scotian Institute, 91 in 1890 and 134 in 1897; the Ottawa Field Naturalists' Club, 168 in 1885 and 300 in 1890. If anything the proportion of those who actively reported discoveries was probably smaller in these societies than in the Nova Scotia case.)

These associations drew their members from a broad cross-section of the educated, urban, middle classes. Among these, medical doctors and pharmacists were always prominent, in part because their training involved a familiarity with the medical uses of plants. Two of the mainstays of the Nova Scotia Institute were medical men – John Sommers, who became an authority on the local mosses and fungi, and Bernard Gilpin, who wrote extensively on the food fishes, mammals, and predatory birds. The London pharmacist William Saunders started out as a druggist and was led into economic entomology through his experiments in cultivating fruit trees. Dr John Christian Schultz, better known as the rabble-rouser of the Canadian party at Red River, collected plants in that troubled district and helped establish the rather premature Scientific Institute of Rupert's Land in 1860. William Brodie, who founded the Natural History Society of Toronto (which was affiliated with the Canadian Institute), practised dentistry.

Equally conspicuous in these groups, especially in Nova Scotia and New Brunswick, were talented British military officers who were drawn to natural history partly out of their zeal for 'sporting zoology.' Leith Adams, a surgeon major with the Twenty-Second (Cheshire) Regiment, was an exceptionally well-informed and acute observer and the author of *Field and Forest Rambles, with Observations on the Natural History of Eastern Canada* (1873). Campbell Hardy of the Royal Artillery carried his devotion to the hunt to extremes when he kept a young moose in his quarters at the Halifax garrison in order to study its habits and character. (It became most affectionate, he reported, when pipe smoke was blown in its face; the beast unfortunately died at the age of two from eating too many turnips.)

For ministers of the gospel, such as Charles Bethune, the founder of the Entomological Society, Robert Campbell, of St Gabriel Street Presbyterian Church in Montreal, and the Free Church cleric David Honeyman, who resigned his charge at Antigonish in order to concentrate upon his monomania, the fossil rocks at Arisaig, ultimately becoming the provincial geologist, the study of nature was almost a religious duty. Educators in the public school system were in the forefront of efforts to secure a more adequate recognition of natural science in the classrooms. Alexander H. MacKay, principal of Pictou Academy from 1873 to 1889 and later superintendent of education for

Nova Scotia, was a fervent advocate of nature study as well as an able botanist. His counterpart in New Brunswick, George U. Hay, editor of the *Educational Record*, shared all his enthusiasms for popularizing natural science, including the more extensive use of native plants in gardens, a teaching that he put into practice on his two- and-a-half-acre estate near Saint John, where he cultivated some 500 species of indigenous flowering plants and ferns.

Among the successful businessmen and lawyers who were listed as honorary patrons of the societies there were only a few practising naturalists. The wealthy lawyer George W. Allen, who was in the mid-1850s mayor of Toronto and president of the Canadian Institute, published an article on his collection of 145 species of local birds and was one of the few Canadians who could afford to subscribe to Audubon's large bird folios. Thomas McIlwraith, a Hamilton fuel dealer and the founder of the Hamilton association of naturalists, customarily arose at four o'clock in the morning to gather the material for his pioneer study, *The Birds of Ontario* (1886).

These circles also contained a sprinkling of clerks, skilled tradesmen, and farmers. The amateur geologist George Matthew, one of the most diligent of fossil-hunters in the 'ferm ledges' near Saint John, was employed as a clerk in the custom-house at that port. William Couper, the entomologist, represented the most intellectually active group among the aristocracy of labour – the printers. The Prince Edward Island farmer Francis Bain, who, with the husband of Lucy Maud Montgomery, had started that province's ephemeral natural history society, contributed a science column to the local press and discovered a fossil-fern later named after him by William Dawson. Among the first members of the London branch of the Entomological Society of Canada were a customs clerk, a cabinet-maker, and an iron-turner.

Since the natural history societies were the earliest organizations of intellectual activity, they attracted individuals who made their mark in fields other than science. The painter Cornelius Krieghoff, who accumulated collections of natural history objects for sale, was a member of the Montreal society in the 1840s. In the 1880s and 1890s the Ottawa Field Naturalists' Club was singularly favoured by the concentration in the capital of cultivated civil servants who joined its ranks and participated in its activities. These included not only nearly all the scientists employed by the government, but also the poet Duncan Campbell Scott, the essayist William Le Sueur, the clerk of the House of Commons and historian John George Bourinot, and Archibald Lampman, whose poetical views of Ottawa, always the city of shimmering spires in the distance, were seen from the favourite haunts of the club in the nearby hills.

Despite the example of Lady Dalhousie, who was more than an ornamental member of the early Quebec society, there were few women in these societies in the early years. At first not admitted at all, later included as associate members ineligible for executive positions, they were treated with condescension. By the 1880s this became a political question, and the sex barrier to membership was broken. The exclusion of women from societies devoted to improving the teaching of science in the schools was becoming impossible as women were coming to dominate elementary school teaching. After the turn of the century the women in these societies vastly outnumbered the men.

The scientific purpose of the societies was to encourage the accumulation of information relating to natural history and, above all, to bring it to the attention of the scientific community through publication. To open the faded and dusty transactions and bulletins – the unfeeling would measure them in yards of library shelving – is to glimpse something of the astonishingly eclectic character of natural history, the unlimited thirst for facts about nature, and the earnestness and touching innocence of the Victorian enthusiasm for science. The typical communication was the description of a new species or the comprehensive inventory, constantly amended and expanded, of objects in a locality or province. The Ottawa Field Naturalists' Club was entirely representative when it declared its mandate to make a systematic exploration of an area within a thirty-mile radius of the city and filled the pages of its journal with notes of birds sighted; lists of mosses, ferns, dragon-flies, flowering plants, molluscs, fossils, and fish; and life histories of the black bear, otter, and deer. The members of the Montreal society in 1861 entertained papers on the swans and geese of Hudson Bay, on the local mammals and birds, and on the land and fresh-water shells collected around lakes Superior and Huron. In the 1860s those in the Saint John society listened to a report on the changes in the colour of the North American hare and to speculations on the antiquity of man and the border between instinct and intelligence in animals. Their contemporaries in Halifax were addressed on the geological formation of the Cobequid Mountains, the dwelling places of the muskrat and the beaver, and studies of the behaviour of rapacious birds. In time the addicted reader no longer finds it surprising that an appraisal of the current state of oyster culture and the announcement of a previously unknown fossil plant follow an essay on whether young loons eat fresh-water clams. These reports of the inventory of nature were often mingled with accounts of human activity and anecdotes concerning the observer as well as the observed.

Though natural history was transacted in facts and details, naturalists were not oblivious to the more general philosophy of scientific inquiry that underlay their activity. When they tried to make these principles explicit they usually prefaced their remarks with approving references to Francis Bacon, who two centuries before had equated an understanding (and hence control) of nature with the patient accumulation of detail, not with deductions from supposedly universal principles. Only apparently innocent of any philosophy of science, these naturalists expected that from the assembly of authenticated facts would in due time emerge, almost automatically, general patterns and unsuspected relations. Thus no specimen was too lowly, no observation too trivial, to be accorded a place in their publications. 'A stray fact may be collected,' ran the common theme, 'or a chance thought evolved, which, however imperfectly turned to account by us, may lead to consequences of which we little dream.'[6] All facts and observations were, therefore, equal, at least provisionally; only the collection of many other facts would determine the ultimate value of any particular one. Natural history, in short, equated growth of scientific knowledge with the accumulation of information.

This altogether engrossing task of collection and amassing information made science accessible and egalitarian; discoveries could be readily understood and contributions of permanent value could be made by part-time amateurs. Previously unknown species, moreover, were customarily named after the individual who discovered them or first described them: in this custom there was the promise for even the humblest naturalist of the ultimate satisfaction of attaining scientific immortality. The compilation of lists or notes of observations also provided an avenue for personal recognition through publication and the circulation of scientific periodicals. The *Bulletin* of the Nova Scotia Institute of Natural Science in 1895 was sent to 734 scientific institutions, libraries, and universities in Britain, the United States, continental Europe, and Canada,[7] and the exchange lists of the *Ottawa Naturalist* or the *Canadian Record of Science* of the Montreal society were at least as extensive. This practice gave to the naturalist a sense of participating in a scientific enterprise that transcended local confines and that brought his discoveries and his name to the attention of an international community.

This concentration upon collecting, moreover, was justified, because so little was known about the natural history of even long-settled districts. Plant life within a small area varies with minor topographical differences; the same is true of the animal, insect, and bird life supported by the flora. Thus a simple inventory of the unique congregations of plants and animals depended upon the efforts of many naturalists and upon observations and collections made continually in the same places over many seasons. Moreover, fossils and remnants of the material cultures of prehistoric peoples were often accidentally exposed in the course of mining, making cuttings for canals and railways, and digging for the foundations for buildings, and this too placed a premium upon knowledgeable collectors being on the spot. Science as inventory was also at the centre of the operations of the Geological Survey, which in 1872 became the Geological and Natural History Survey and was charged with making collections in all departments of natural science throughout the immense territories acquired by the new Dominion. As late as 1890, the director of the Survey, George M. Dawson, noted that of Canada's total territory of some three and a half million square miles, between one-quarter and one-third remained unmapped and unexplored in even the most superficial fashion. The enormous task of reconnoitring this territory served to reinforce within Canada's major scientific institution a focus upon science as collection and description.[8]

This type of scientific work provided a common basis of understanding and a close link between amateurs in the natural history societies and professional geologists, some of whom possessed university degrees and were employed full time in government service. It was possible for able and self-taught amateurs to make the transition to full-time professional employment. James Fletcher, who came to Canada in the service of the Bank of British North America and later joined the staff of the Library of Parliament, acquired a knowledge of botany and insect life in his spare time, became Dominion Entomologist in 1884, and from 1887 to 1908 served as entomologist and botanist to the Dominion Experimental Farm. John Macoun experienced a similar transition, both professionally and socially. A self-taught naturalist, an enthusiast to the point of self-caricature, Macoun gained favourable public notice for his western explorations and notoriety for his optimistic forecasts about the suitability of the southern prairie lands for agriculture – assessments based on the character of plant life rather than analysis of the soil or measurement of rainfall. Appointed botanist to the Geological Survey in 1882, he was five years later made Dominion Naturalist and instructed to acquire comprehensive collections, first of plants, later of birds, and finally nearly everything. Except for the territorial scope of his operations, there was little about his practice of science that separated him from those amateurs from whose ranks he had come.

The popularization of the culture of science was at least as prominent in the agenda of societies as the accumulation of information. They sponsored conversaziones, or social occasions, for the discussion of science. Some 200 people attended one at the Horticultural Hall in Halifax in July 1865 to listen to an address by the president of the Nova Scotian Institute of Natural Science and papers on butterflies and moths of the colony, on the process of smoking the Digby herring, and on the geology of the Halifax district. After an interval during which ices, lemonade, strawberries and cream, and cakes were served, the audience regrouped to hear further remarks on botany and concluding remarks by the president![9] Social evenings at which the public was invited to view microscopic slides, observe chemical demonstrations, or inspect the holdings of the museum or specially arranged collections – interspersed by lectures or the music of military bands – were regular features of the larger societies, in Montreal and Ottawa. In an age when hours of leisure not devoted to self-improvement hung heavily on the evangelical conscience and when there were so few acceptable alternative amusements, the natural history society combined in its appeal both sociability and instruction.

Of all the tactics devised to broaden the appeal of natural science, the most attractive was the field excursion, a more organized form of the individual naturalist's ramble through the countryside. Begun in the 1860s by the Halifax and Montreal clubs, these excursions combined the study of nature with the pleasures of the picnic and healthy outdoor exercise. On its first spring outing in May 1879, 42 members of the Ottawa Field Naturalists' Club and their friends travelled by van to Kingsmere, viewed and sketched the surrounding scenery from King's Mountain, and collected a variety of specimens, the prizes being two luna moths. (The only mishap occurred when one man stumbled on a log and, falling on his pocket, crushed a glass bottle full of beetles.) Subsequent field excursions were more structured: members were organized into sections according to their special interests, each branch directed by a leader, usually someone from the Geological Survey or the Experimental Farm, who directed collecting parties and gave a talk at the end of the day on the significance of what had been seen and collected. Prizes were awarded to the best collections in each department and for additions to the lists. In the 1880s and 1890s these outings made the Ottawa club one of the most successful in the country: in 1902 some 300 people, including most of the students from the normal school, took part in the expedition to Chelsea.

Combining sociability with science, the natural history societies occupied a curious, transitional position both in the organization of Canadian science and in the hierarchy of scientific authority. Localistic both in their preoccupation with making better known the resources of particular districts and in the allegiances of their members, they failed to transcend their origins and form a scientific community of national scope.[10] Not until the formation of the Royal Society in 1882 did Canada acquire a national focus for scientific activity: this took place belatedly, a half-century after the organization of the British Association for the Advancement of Science (1831) and a generation after the American Association for the Advancement of Science (1848), and was initiated by the governor-general, the marquis of Lorne, as part of his personal scheme to promote Canadian cultural life. Though many, including Sir John A. Macdonald, thought of the Royal Society as a scientific institution, it was a literary society as well. In addition to section III, comprising the geological and biological sciences, and section IV, devoted to mathematics and the chemical and physical sciences, it encompassed French- and English-language branches in history and literature. The feature of the new society that most clearly differentiated it from both the local societies and the British and American national associations was that it was to admit, by invitation, only men of recognized merit and achievement. The original members of the two scientific sections numbered forty; in contrast, the Australian Association for the Advancement of Science, founded in 1886 and open to anyone, professional or amateur, who had a serious interest in science, started with 820.[11] The Canadian society very early took on the aura of the established and – to youthful critics – the old. (Of the 1894 meeting Archibald Lampman wrote: 'The dry bones gave forth a vivacious rattle.'[12]) Unlike the British association, which met annually in different cities, the Royal Society conducted its gatherings in Ottawa, a custom that isolated it from the centres in which the local societies flourished.

The formation and early years of the Royal Society illuminated two important features in the intellectual landscape of Victorian Canada. The first is the relative status of the scientific and literary cultures. In the process of selecting the first members, Dawson, who was Lord Lorne's main adviser on these matters, had some difficulty in finding men of sufficient standing. In the sciences the problem was relatively simple: as Daniel Wilson said, the very humblest naturalist 'may contribute some new fact or observation in Science that will have its value ... But what is proposed or expected that the Section on English Literature is to do? Shall we write school-boy essays, or criticisms on the literature of the day; or theses on the want of literature?' 'I know not who to name,' he told Dawson in exasperation. 'It is like making bricks not only without straw, but without clay. However I shall try and make out a list of illustrious nobodies; the more insignificant they may be, the higher will be their delights when such Honours are thrust upon them.'[13] Wilson's standards were exacting but not unrealistic or severe. It was less difficult to secure external recognition for natural history and geology than for literary work.

The early years show, second, that scientific activity in Victorian Canada was sustained and dominated by English Canadians and that support for science in French Canada was feeble and marginal to that community's intellectual interests. This had not always been the case: in the early 1830s French Canadians constituted one-third of the membership of the Literary and Historical Society of Quebec, though they were content to leave the preparation of articles on geology and natural history to the English and then withdrew during the ethnic turmoil that preceded the rebellions. The Montreal Natural History Society, the major institution in the province, was created by the minority and resolutely remained an English-Canadian preserve. The instituts canadiens, which drew their followers from the same professional classes that in English Canada supplied so many amateur naturalists, seldom displayed more than the most general and intermittent interest in natural science, preferring instead lectures on literature and patriotic history. The published naturalists of French Canada could be counted almost on the fingers of one hand: they were usually priests, such as Abbé Léon Provancher, who edited and wrote most of *Le Naturaliste canadien*, published between 1868 and 1891.

This pattern of unequal support for science was inevitably reflected in the ethnic composition of the Royal Society. Of the first twenty members of the geology and biology section only two were French Canadians – D.N. St Cyr and J.C.K. Laflamme; by 1900 this section had twenty-seven fellows, but only Laflamme represented French Canada. In 1900 section IV listed twenty-seven names; only three were French. When the society was first organized, French-Canadian men of letters insisted upon two separate literary and historical sections based on language lines; they seemed content to leave the scientific departments to English Canadians.[14] Insofar as the Royal Society accurately reflected the state of achievement as well as the enthusiasm for the sciences, these figures seem almost a caricature of the then current myth that to the French belonged the artistic, literary, and spiritual side of intellectual effort, and to the materialistic Anglo-Saxons belonged the monopoly of commerce, finance, and science.

Provancher was an outstanding exception to this pattern, because of his recognized contributions to botany and entomology and his extensive connections with naturalists in the United States and continental Europe; but he was also bound up in the same web of influences that inhibited natural history in French Canada. One theme that runs through all his writings is an appeal for a greater appreciation of science, particularly natural science, among his compatriots. The attention devoted to the pursuit and study of this subject was for him the measure of the state of civilization of a people, and by this test he judged French Canada shamefully deficient. He attributed this to inadequate teaching of science in the schools and classical colleges and drew unflattering comparisons between the failure of the Council of Agriculture of Quebec to employ or take the advice of qualified entomologists and the situation in Ontario. Provancher also recognized the bias of the educational system, the tendency of the educated élite to concentrate upon careers in the church, law, or medicine, and the disregard for other professions, including scientific ones.[15] While he peppered his journal with condemnations of such obstacles to an appreciation of science in Quebec, he could respond to slights or implied criticisms from outsiders in a protective, defensive manner. This priest was a prickly *nationaliste* who loved natural history in and for itself but what he wanted for Quebec was a French-language society – open to all but with the official language French.[16] It may be for reasons such as these that he at first refused to join the Royal Society though he relented later.

The world of the English-Canadian naturalists, despite the self-conscious patriotism that lay back of the creation of the Royal Society, was international. 'The great physical laws of the universe are the same in all lands,' ran a typical assertion about the cosmopolitanism of science. 'Geological structure and animal and vegetable life are everywhere framed on one uniform type. We cannot attempt to nationalize science without losing its greatest results.'[17] The revelation of natural history was inescapably a collective enterprise in which information was shared and specimens were dispatched to be identified and classified by authorities who had access to type collections and libraries. It was to be expected that British-born immigrants, who were so conspicuous in colonial natural history, should send their finds to the Royal Botanic Garden at Kew or to the British Museum, publish their discoveries in the journals of the homeland, and continue to look to Britain for recognition through election to prestigious societies or honours from the crown.

After the middle years of the century, this imperial connection was supplemented by the development of associations with the United States that grew ever more intimate and substantial. Natural history south of the border was a more highly developed field of study, and descriptions by Americans of natural forms belonging to a common environment had a compelling interest for Canadians. The publications of American scientists and the reports of their societies, institutions, and surveys were eagerly acquired by purchase or exchange by Canadian organizations; Canadian botanists such as Macoun or Provancher looked to Asa Gray of Harvard as the authority in their field; and entomologists often resorted to the discriminating judgments of S.H. Scudder of Cambridge, Massachusetts. Naturalists of the Dominion joined American organizations (at least 135 Canadians were members of the American Association for the Advancement of Science in 1857),[18] published in American periodicals, and invited Americans to become corresponding members of their own societies.[19] It says much for the place of Canada in the North Atlantic triangle of science that William Dawson was the only person to become president of both the British and the American associations.

In some areas the influence of American initiatives came to overshadow if not totally displace the older imperial links. After mid-century the Smithsonian Institution in Washington, DC, founded in 1846 (with funds from the bequest of an Englishman), became, under the energetic direction of assistant secretary Spencer Baird, a dominant presence in the Hudson's Bay Company's territories. In 1859, with the full support and co-operation of the company, Robert Kennicott of the Smithsonian began his travels through the northwest and into Russian America and ignited an enthusiasm among fur-traders for collecting natural history specimens and compiling observations. It was Baird, however, who by cajolery and presents – scientific reports, preserving alcohol, even novels and poetry – sustained their zeal and ensured the flow of shipments of birds and mammals, eggs, notes on life histories, Eskimo relics, meteorological records, and even information on the fluctuations of animal populations based on district fur returns. In his appeals to these officers, isolated in the wilderness but by their trade familiar with animal life, Baird offered them some purposeful activity that would ensure their names a place in the annals of science. In the early 1860s he received collections from some twenty Hudson's Bay Company officers – including Donald Smith in Labrador, William MacTavish, governor of Assiniboia, Roderick MacFarlane and Bernard Ross, in the Mackenzie district, and George Barnston, then stationed on Lake Superior.[20] While the Smithsonian was the chief beneficiary of the growth of knowledge about vast territories that Canada was only beginning to see as her own inheritance, these initiatives did not entirely obliterate the older associations. But one must wonder what the members of the Natural History Society of Montreal felt when they learned that the best specimens collected in the northwest were retained in Washington and that unwanted duplicates were sent on to them. (Even the network for exchanging Canadian publications with centres abroad was organized through the Smithsonian.)

Some aspects of the work of John Macoun as Dominion Naturalist offer in microcosm further illustrations of this growing collaboration with American naturalists and also some additional reasons for it. Responsible for organizing comprehensive collections of the botany of Canada, Macoun lived an annual routine of summers devoted to field work and winters in Ottawa cataloguing and classifying, organizing the Geological Survey's museum, arranging exchanges with individuals and institutions, and conducting an extensive correspondence with experts who identified his specimens. During thirty summers Macoun penetrated into nearly every accessible district of Canada, assembled a collection of more than 100,000 specimens, and issued in instalments two important publications, *Catalogue of Canadian Plants* (between 1883 and 1906) and *Catalogue of Canadian Birds* (in 1900, 1903, and 1904).

Macoun occupied a curious position on the ladder of scientific authority. Recognized as Canada's foremost botanist – 'Canada's Linnaeus' – he regularly identified collections sent to him by amateur naturalists. He could be encouraging, and he could be testy, reprimanding them for lack of care in preparing specimens or for the use of outdated names. In his dealings with experts abroad, however, he was uncomplaining and deferential. He was above all a field naturalist and had little aptitude for specialized study; by temperament a collector, his greatest moments of satisfaction came from finding a plant never obtained before. He was responsible for covering the whole country and worked some of the time in fields in which his duties as well as his ambitions exceed his knowledge; he simply spread himself too thin. 'I have no time for critical examination,' he once complained, 'and must hand my material over to others.' 'I was quite successful,' he wrote of one journey, '... and obtained many fine things but being a collector of everything I did not distinguish myself particularly in anything. I managed however to collect many specimens of various forms some of which are unique.'[21] This judgment could well describe his career.

Thus Macoun cultivated, and became very dependent upon, expert correspondents. In the 1860s he had dispatched collections to Asa Gray at Harvard and William J. Hooker at Kew, though he later lost patience with the British for their slowness. For over two years, he once wrote in a huff, he awaited some response from the Natural History Museum in South Kensington to acknowledge his shipment of algae. 'So do not blame us if we look to the Americans in preference to you.'[22] For his inventory of plants, Macoun was indebted to many people, especially to the Swede N.C. Kindberg and the German Carl Müller, who identified his mosses.

His dependence was accentuated, moreover, by the shifting and confusing standards for classifying and naming plants and by the contradictory tendencies of splitting, making distinct species out of varieties, and lumping, or designating substantially different specimens under one name. In the debates on classification that upset the botanical world, Macoun stood on the sidelines, sometimes bemused and bewildered, often irritated, particularly by younger men who set out to revise entire classification systems but who 'have not lived as long as I have spent in the field.'[23] Instinctively Macoun preferred the traditional and settled order, though he had more sympathy with those who erred in making too many species than with those who made too few. His own reputation as a botanist was tied up with new discoveries that only experts could authenticate. Kindberg and Müller credited him with 171 species of mosses that had never been described – fully one-fifth of the moss flora of North America. Macoun knew that they were excessively liberal in their judgments, but the results were pleasing to his vanity.

He testified (saying more perhaps than he realized), 'I am satisfied to collect and discriminate generally, but I will not destroy my eyes by working with a microscope.'

When Macoun turned from botany to the systematic collection of birds and mammals he sought the advice of Americans who were concerned with biology in continental terms and became even more reliant upon many whose level of specialization exceeded his own. The key figure for him, as for other Canadian naturalists, was C. Hartt Merriam, who was in charge of economic ornithology and mammalogy in the United States Department of Agriculture (after 1896 this branch became the Biological Survey). Merriam was also the chairman of the committee on bird migration of the American Ornithologists' Union, which had been established, with the help of some Canadians, in 1883. The purpose of this committee was not merely to note the presence of species in certain areas, but to elicit any information bearing upon migration – storms, temperature changes, and the dates of the appearance of insects. Necessarily continental in scope and dependent upon the observations of a large number of naturalists on both sides of the border, this program enlisted the support of Canada's practising ornithologists – James LeMoine in Quebec, Montague Chamberlain in New Brunswick, Thomas McIlwraith in Ontario, and young Ernest Thompson Seton in Manitoba. Merriam's collaboration with Macoun was especially close, for he required all the information he could find about the range and breeding habits of birds and the distribution of the mammals of northern America. For his part, Macoun depended upon Merriam for aid in identifications, for advice about collecting, and for contacts with others in fields in which neither was expert. Merriam not only instructed Macoun on how to collect, but also told him what to look for and where to go![24]

Macoun's experience provides a striking instance of the continuing dependence upon external authority; it also exemplifies the degree to which naturalists of his generation helped create the basis of scientific institutions and began the indispensable preliminary outline of Canada's natural features. Natural history matured in the late nineteenth century as naturalists in the country defined, at least in part, their own objectives. Their achievement was visible in the collections in nearly every provincial capital; in the National Museum, opened in Ottawa in 1910 and aptly dedicated to the memory of Queen Victoria; and in the growing number of reports and bulletins published by government agencies, the Royal Society, and the local societies. Theirs was a partial, modest accomplishment; it seemed prosaic, reported in a language that suppressed the pleasure and excitement that entered into it.

The organization of science was local, national, and international. So intimate were the ties of correspondence and exchange that linked naturalists in Canada, Britain, and the United States that there must be few other aspects of Canada's intellectual life that better exemplified the common culture of the North Atlantic triangle. This pattern grew out of the very logic of science defined as inventory: it also coincided with the engrained preferences of British North Americans. The organization of science bore an uncanny resemblance to the political culture in which it was conducted: the vigorous localism of the societies and the ineffectuality of the Royal Society as a co-ordinating centre paralleled the counter-pulls of provincialism and centralization in politics. The world of science duplicated also the Canadian blend of local autonomy and continuing participation in the imperial system.

To dwell on these institution patterns no doubt indirectly attests to the vitality of natural history, but it misses something essential about the Victorian view of nature and the appeal of natural history. That appeal rested upon a religious basis and a comforting view of man's place in nature, and it is to this that I shall turn in the second lecture.

2

God

NATURAL HISTORY WAS more than the collection of facts and more than societies for the promotion of science; it was also a way of seeing, a sensibility, and a medium for communicating something essential about nature and man's place in it. Of the practical utility of science naturalists wrote much, for they were seeking support from a colonial society that was suspicious of the theoretical and ornamental and insistent on the directly useful; they spoke less frequently but no less eloquently of its pleasures and enchantments. Natural history blended scientific accuracy and a rigid factualism with a sense of wonder and a celebration of mystery; aesthetic and religious appreciation entered into its practice and its justification. The study of living things no doubt has its own enduring fascination, but Victorians saw in nature what they were instructed to see – the work of God.

The study of nature had been invested with a theological significance in Britain, perhaps more than in any other country, since the seventeenth century, and this tradition – natural theology – went generally unchallenged until the later Victorian period. It found its most persuasive expression in John Ray's *The Wisdom of God Manifested in the Works of Creation* (1691), which celebrated the power of the Deity in the sheer number of living things no less than in the grandeur of the heavens and commended the pursuit of science as a religious exercise. It was illustrated in a classic of enduring popularity, *The Natural History of Selborne* (1789) by the parson and naturalist Gilbert White. It was restated by William Paley in 1802 in an influential book with an equally expressive title, *Natural Theology; or, Evidence of the Existence and Attributes of the Deity Collected from the Appearances of Nature*. The notion of science devoted to the revelation of the activity and plans of God in nature was made familiar to generations of Victorians in Britain and North America either directly through these works or indirectly through popularizations written especially for Canadians.[1] The chief themes of natural theology were ritualized in prefaces to natural history publications, embroidered upon in sermons, and vulgarized in children's stories that invariably represented nature hand in hand with good behaviour. So intimately intertwined were natural history and religious considerations that it was inconceivable to study nature without reference to a higher power. The chief claim of natural theology was that there existed an overall design in nature, a rank and order in the chain of life, and a regularity in the operation of laws, all of which were evidence of a transcendent guiding intelligence. For theologians, these truths became abstract arguments for the existence of God; for naturalists they offered a religious sanction for scientific investigation. Nature was worth studying because it was a product of divine activity; since God created everything, the more intricate the patterns discovered, the more testimony there was to his wisdom and artistry. Thus natural science enlarged man's comprehension of God's works and intentions just as theology revealed the laws of salvation in scripture. Natural theology gave to natural history a legitimacy and status in Victorian evangelical culture that went beyond practical utility.

These religious considerations not only figured prominently in justifications for the study of nature but also directed the attention of naturalists into particular channels. They were especially concerned with adaptation in nature, with the ways in which organisms had been exquisitely fitted by the skilful contriver for the places they occupied. Entirely representative of this approach was the reaction of John Keast Lord, naturalist with the British North American boundary commission, to discovering a tiny mole-like creature on the western slopes of the Cascade Mountains. This curious animal possessed a snout lengthened out into a cylindrical tube; it had no eyes and only rudimentary ears and lived exclusively in tunnels in the earth. 'When we contemplate this grotesque and strangely-formed little creature,' Lord exclaimed, 'and see how wisely and wonderfully it is fashioned and adapted to its destined place, supplying another missing link in the great chain of Nature, we cannot but feel God's

power and omnipresence.'[2] Natural history, moreover, reinforced attention upon interrelationships in concrete terms and
upon the fact that nothing in the natural world was useless or
without purpose. One of the many reasons for the continuing
appeal of Gilbert White's *Natural History of Selborne* was his
charming description of one small place filled with an astonishing number of creatures, each playing a role in nature's economy, and all interlinked in chains of mutual dependence. White
wrote of earthworms that areated the soil for man's benefit and
of cattle cooling themselves in ponds, providing by their drop-
pings food for insects and, indirectly, for fish. Such observations
as these, which illustrated the essential interdependence in
nature, have led more than one historian to conclude that natural theology possessed a real feeling for the web of life and a
sense of what another age would redefine and call ecology.[3] Early
Victorian natural history highlighted adaptation and interrelationships: it described organisms that had come into being at the
creation or at successive creations and were assumed to be permanent and fixed. The naturalist no more considered inquiring
into the origin of species than his seventeenth-century predeces-
sor thought of speculating upon the origins of gravitation.

The belief that religious insight could be acquired from the
study of nature equated science with an act of worship and
coloured perceptions of its laws and facts. To describe species
and understand their adaptations to their environments, was to
touch directly upon something holy and sacred. The facts of natural history were not arid, isolated and neutral; they were invested with a mystery and reverence. 'A physical fact,' said the
American naturalist Louis Agassiz, 'is as sacred as a moral principle.' The Victorian naturalist studied nature and ended by discovering marvels.

One of the main literary strategies of naturalists who sought to
communicate their insights to a general audience was to fix
upon a closely observed detail in nature, convey their own awe

and wonder, and create a mood of veneration. This was the purpose of the first popular account of Canadian natural history, *The Canadian Naturalist* (1840), by Philip Henry Gosse, who felt that the hand of God was as much a guiding force in personal life as in nature. According to his own account, in 1832, while working as a clerk in the office of a fish merchant in Carbonear, he bought (from a Methodist minister) a ten-shilling book that made him a naturalist and a Christian. After this conversion, he became obsessed with a life of perfect self-abnegation and purity; he also taught himself natural history and, in almost totally unpropitious circumstances, began a systematic study of Newfoundland entomology.[4] In 1835 he purchased a farm near Compton, in the Eastern Townships of Quebec, and though he left after three disappointing years he came to know the natural scene of the district intimately. His book, written in emulation of Gilbert White, reported conversations between a rather domineering father and his dull and uninformed son on their walks through the countryside at various seasons of the year.

Some of the enthusiasm, scrupulous attention to detail, and gift of direct description that later made Gosse one of the most widely read of all British naturalists was evident in this early book; so too were the hints of that harsh arrogance of Christian humility that his son was to disclose in one of the most devastating of family memoirs. There was a freshness in his evocation of wonder at things they observed – the northern lights and the forms of snowflakes, the mystery of bird migration, the multiple lenses of the eyes of a fly. Even something so obscure as the tail of a dragon-fly grub, which enabled it to move and live, filled Gosse with unbounded admiration for the being that contrived it.

Apart from his obvious resolution to stimulate an appreciation for the joys of natural history, Gosse's aim was to demonstrate, as he put it, that nature 'is never barren of lessons of wisdom to him who possesses a mind willing to receive them.' 'This fact cannot be too strongly impressed,' he emphasized. 'We must not rest in the creature but be led up to the Creator.'[5] From the marvels of nature and the specific examples of contrivance up the chain of being to God was the route of thought and feeling that his book was intended to stimulate and direct. And the lessons of wisdom that the study of nature confirmed were the familiar truisms: the variety of creatures so perfectly adapted to their situations revealed a skilled designer; there was no place in nature, however small and inhospitable, that did not sustain some form of life; and nature was governed by a generally benevolent, caring creator.

This comforting message was reaffirmed by Catherine Parr Traill in many stories, essays, and, above all, in *Studies of Plant Life in Canada*, a splendid anachronism, published in 1885 when she was eighty-three, and which belonged, at least in its natural theology, to the time of her youth. A diligent, pietistic botanist, Traill exemplified the view that nature was a theatre of religious ideas and feelings. She belonged to a class of English gentlefolk for whom a familiarity with plant life and the art of botanical illustration was considered a desirable accomplishment of the educated woman. This idea was upheld by Queen Victoria and, in Canada, by Maria Morris, who published a series of folios of paintings of the flowers of Nova Scotia, and by Agnes Fitzgibbon, Traill's niece, who painted and lithographed ten large plates for *Canadian Wild Flowers* (1868).[6] Traill's passion for botany also grew out of first-hand pioneer experience. In her guides for female immigrants she drew upon an extensive knowledge, gleaned from the Indians and older settlers, of the uses of wild plants for food, tonics, herbal remedies, and dyes. She wrote too out of desperate financial necessity. Her life was dogged by setbacks and misfortunes that would have destroyed the optimism and stifled the creativity of a less resilient person. The early death of her husband, the burning of her home, and desperate poverty compelled her to publish manuals and children's stories and to compile folios of dried plants for sale. There was about her character a 'practical solidity,'[7] an inner strength that came from a faith in God's direction. For Traill, as for Gosse, the conventions of natural theology were not mere figures of speech but the sources of spiritual comfort.

Traill's botany was at once scientific and literary. In *Studies*, which was based upon almost half a century of observation, she described more than 200 flowering plants, as well as trees, shrubs, and ferns, in terms of appearance, location, and habits of growth. Praised for her accuracy of characterization,[8] she was as much concerned with the aesthetic aspects of plants and with their mystical connections with human life as she was with orthodox natural history. She arranged her accounts of plants in the order that an observer might encounter them in the fields and woods rather than in the categories of scientific classification, and she preferred their common over their scientific names because of their association with folklore and their literary echoes in Shakespeare, Milton, and William Cullen Bryant. Like all romantics, Traill sought not merely to depict what she saw, but to convey her own emotional responses to nature. Hers was the spirit of the immigrant, an exile, living in a strange country where the woods were so astonishingly silent and the months of March and April so desolate. The sight of a familiar flower – similar though not identical to those she had known in England – triggered twinges of nostalgia and the feeling of loss. Yet because of the resemblances they provided reassurances and comfort too. The cycles of growth and the transitoriness of flowers became for Traill metaphors for human destiny, underlining the fragility of life but also offering proof of a caring providence.

Plant life carried moral teachings and testified to the general beneficence of God's arrangements. The operations of nature were co-operative and graceful, all pointing to a creative love and caring that Traill called a 'maternal instinct.' She found this in the way in which the spore of a fern was protected, in what she termed the 'law of mutual dependence' in the relations of plants, and in the astonishing fecundity of nature. 'There seems to me,' she wrote, in lines that could have been taken from Gilbert White or any of his Victorian imitators, '... no space unfilled in God's creation. Something fills up all vacancies, either in vegetable or animal life; unseen organisms, too subtle and too fine to be visible to our unassisted vision, have their existence though we behold them not.' Nature appeared to be the mirror image of the ideal Victorian evangelical – never wasteful, always busy, incredibly productive: 'So beautiful is the arrangement of God's economy in the vegetable world that something gathers up all fragments and nothing is lost.' The teaching communicated by the flowers was that 'His tender care is over all His works': this was a simple lesson, accessible to all, and one that by stimulating a feeling for the benevolence of providence prepared the mind to receive the gospel of salvation.[9]

Gosse and Traill were popular writers: while using original details gathered from Canadian natural history, they tried to convey at a common level of understanding a view of nature that was commonplace in Britain. Their books also show how this kind of natural history became almost a form of confessional literature that attested to their authors' deeply felt religious convictions as well as to their curiosity about nature. Significantly, neither of them mentioned geology, a science that matured quickly in the first half of the century and presented problems for those who tried to maintain the correspondence between biblical teachings and natural history. It was left to William Dawson to bring out, at a different level of sophistication, the essential harmony of revelation and the findings of the new science of the earth.

By the 1830s geologists had arrived at a consensus about patterns in the development of the earth and the fossil series. The world was very old, its history measured in millions of years; that history consisted of a succession of distinct epochs represented by formations that contained the remnants or imprints of unique assemblages of animals and plants; each of these ages had been swept away in processes of mass extinction. Authorities agreed that the successive appearance of fish, amphibians, reptiles, marsupials, mammals, and finally man, and the parallel sequence towards more complex forms of plant life, displayed progressive development that could be attributed to the creative will, operating either directly or through natural laws. What was left in doubt and remained in dispute for some time was how the major types of animals and plants had come into existence and what agencies had operated to bring about geological change. In *The Principles of Geology* (1830) Charles Lyell proposed that such changes in the history of the earth could be attributed not to spectacular catastrophes of flood or fire but to the operation of causes of the same kind and degree as could still be observed in the silting of rivers, the erosion of mountains, and the rise and fall of the land. The net effect of Lyell's uniformitarianism was to relegate divine intervention to a remote, almost dispensable role in geology and to call into question the whole idea of progressive change.[10]

How these findings were to be accommodated into the Christian understanding of God's supervision of nature and interpreted in terms of the succinct account of creation given in the verses of Genesis became matters of great concern and generated a considerable volume of literature. At one extreme, the Scottish editor Robert Chambers had anonymously published in 1844 the notorious *Vestiges of the Natural History of Creation*, in which he made the case that the fossil record could be explained by a natural law of development of species from preceding forms. This notion of transmutation was universally denounced; far more acceptable, as well as more popular with the educated public, was the reconciliation of geology and scripture offered by another Scot, Hugh Miller, in *The Footprints of the Creator* (1847) and *The Testimony of the Rocks* (1857). In the North Atlantic world Miller enjoyed huge literary success.[11]

Though Dawson owed much to Miller, his own approach to this problem was informed by his considerable experience as a geologist and his abiding belief in a supervisory providence. A friend of Lyell, Dawson had earned his scientific reputation with an extended study of the minerals and formations of the Maritimes and for his account of the flora and land animals that had once lived in the luxuriant forests and lagoons of the Carboniferous period, the age in which the coal measures had been laid down. With Lyell he had disinterred from the upright fossil trees at Joggins on the Cumberland Basin the remains of a lizard-like animal, the first indication that reptiles had lived in the coal period in North America. When he wrote of the consistencies of geology and scripture he did so not simply as a popularizer but as one thoroughly familiar with intricate details of geological science. Also a close student of scripture, he was filled with admiration for the poetical description of nature in the Bible and was convinced that an understanding of science was essential for the interpretation of God's word. It was, he was fond of saying, a barren and fruitless science that sees the work but not its author and a narrow piety that loves God but not his works. Deeply embedded in Dawson's outlook was a Calvinistic sense of a supervisory agency constantly intervening in the lives of individuals. What others might describe as luck or chance he felt as the unmistakable interposition of providence in human affairs. No one will ever understand his scientific thinking who does not recognize that for Dawson this view of life, which balanced free will with predetermination, was as real as anything in material nature.[12]

Like others who aspired to correlate scripture and geology, Dawson, in his *Archaia; or, Studies of the Cosmology and Natural History of the Hebrew Scriptures* (published in 1860, when he was forty), began by repudiating the notion of any disharmony between the two on the grounds that nature and revelation were the products of the same author. The resolution of apparent inconsistencies mainly involved the removal of misunderstandings surrounding scripture, correcting translations, and also drawing only the most scrupulous and responsible inferences from science.[13] Scripture offered only the most general account of creation and was addressed to ancient Hebrews in a language they could comprehend and in terms of their perspective and available information. The Bible was not therefore a treatise on science, even though it clearly presented two essential truths about nature later confirmed by science – that everything served an end and that everything was regulated by natural laws instituted by the creator. Indeed it seemed that God created nature, endowed man with certain faculties, and had positively invited him to study his works.

Though it would be unprofitable and wearisome to retrace all the bypaths by which Dawson illustrated the conjunction of geology and Genesis, two points about his strategy of argument should be noted. One of his favourite explanatory tactics was to enlist his rather formidable command of the Hebrew language in order to define key words in such a way that difficulties in his argument were removed. He had done this before in examining the contradictory teachings of the Bible on the use of wine and strong drink, concluding that those who regulated their conduct by the word of God should abstain;[14] now he dealt in a similar fashion with such words as create and day and explained to his own satisfaction how there could be light on the first day before the sun had been created or how there could be plants without rain.

The central section of his argument – which he took from Miller – was the case that the six days of creation were not limited to twenty-four hours; the days referred to in Genesis were metaphors for protracted periods that corresponded to geological ages or groups of geological eras. Both Genesis and geology attested to the same plan in nature: to the periodic introduction of species fixed in character and a constant elevation along a graduated scale of life upward to the appearance of man.

Just as Lyell's geology had necessitated a more explicit elaboration of the scriptural account, so too contemporary developments in the study of human cultures had to be harmonized with Christian teachings regarding man's origin. From the earliest days of exploration, Europeans had been fascinated by the bewildering variety of human cultures encountered in the New World and had wondered how the first inhabitants came to be there, whether they had been separately created or been changed by the environment. Since the Bible spoke of only one creation, the native peoples were commonly regarded as descendants of migrants from the original centre of man's first existence. When the Literary and Historical Society of Quebec in the 1820s set about collecting accounts of the customs as well as the artefacts of the native races, it did so partly out of sheer romantic antiquarianism, and partly because of the bearing of this information upon the larger issue of demonstrating their Asiatic origin. (One member supported this idea by noting the persistence of a peculiar custom – that North American Indian males, like orientals, adopted the female position while urinating.[15])

The collection of information on the customs, arts, burial sites, and specimens of primitive man became, no less than the collection of plants, animals, and fossils, a central concern of the natural history societies very early and remained so throughout the century. This interest was especially pronounced among the members of the Canadian Institute, one of whom directed attention to the small and diminishing numbers of the race and reminded his audience: 'The time may not be far remote when posterity may be counting its last remnants, and wishing that we in our day had been more alive to the facts and more industrious in setting up marks by which they might measure the ebbing tide, and comprehend the destiny about to be consummated.'[16] There was a widespread acceptance that Indian societies were soon to fade away, just like the native plants. This gave to the task of collecting artefacts and legends a sense of pressing urgency.

There were two other reasons why the cultures of the native peoples commanded attention in the middle decades of the century. Discoveries in Britain and France of man-made weapons and other instruments in conjunction with the remains of extinct animals suggested that northern Europe had been occupied by human populations earlier that had been assumed, and certainly before the five or six thousand years that had been calculated from scripture.

A far more immediate challenge to traditional views came from a group of writers in the United States, especially Samuel G. Morton, George R. Gliddon, Josiah G. Nott, and Louis Agassiz, who explicitly questioned the notion of a common origin of the human race. Attempting to explain the diversity of human types – and living in a society in which northern Europeans, blacks, and Indians lived in 'uneasy conjunction' – they contended that races were distinct species with permanent structures and instincts, separately created in different parts of the earth.[17] (As in other areas of natural history, the fact that these races were so well adapted to the places or zoological provinces in which they were originally found was taken as additional evidence of the creator's skilful contrivance). Racial differences indicated by skin colour, type of hair, and by the shape and facial angles of skulls could be accounted for only by separate creation or by variation from a common ancestry over a very long period of time.

Dawson rejected both of these possibilities for religious and scientific reasons. The Bible knew only one species of man and revelation promised salvation to all. 'The religious tendency of this doctrine,' Dawson wrote of the idea of multiple creation, or polygenesis, 'no Christian can fail to perceive ... It ... destroys the brotherhood of man and the universality of that Christian atonement which proclaims that "as in Adam all die, so in Christ shall all be made alive." '[18] 'The whole question of sin and redemption is bound up with the Unity of the Human Race,' explained a Protestant minister who made more explicit two other hateful implications of polygenesis: it justified the abomination of human slavery, and it undermined the Christian commission to carry the word of God to all peoples.[19]

Though Dawson accepted a long time span for geological history he refused to admit that mankind had existed for more than a few thousand years. The chronology of human history could not be established on the basis of human skulls and tools and the remains of extinct animals, he argued, because animals had been known to become extinct in fairly recent times and the differences between these prehistoric skulls and those of modern Europeans were no greater than the differences between the skulls of northern Europeans and those of North American Indians of his day.

Dawson's case was supported by his friend Daniel Wilson. Wilson, who had written on the archaelogy and prehistoric artefacts of Scotland before he emigrated, in Canada turned his attention to Indian life in the hope that parallel studies of civilizations in the New World and the Old would illuminate what was shared and universal and what was local and unique. As early as 1857 he set out, as he told Dawson, to assail the American dogma that a single head type was to be found throughout the so-called North American Indian race:[20] the skull forms that he had examined, he reported, had been altered by burial rites, diet, environment, and deliberate deformation. Wilson did not challenge the idea that racial groups could be identified with particular head forms; he merely pointed out how difficult such analysis was. Only much later did he reject the notion of cranial capacity as a measurement of the intellectual ability of races.[21] Dawson too did not believe it possible to categorize races on the basis of skull shapes, for these varied too much even within small groups of people.

At the centre of this dispute over multiple creation and distinct races lay the problem of what a species was and how it was to be defined. Naturalists in the 1850s, before Darwin, were fully aware of the arguments for evolution or transmutation that had been made by the Frenchman Lamarck or, more recently and anonymously, by Robert Chambers, and they were united in denouncing them. Like most of their contemporaries, Dawson and Wilson considered species immutable but subject to variation, and they defined a species in terms of interbreeding – two species could not interbreed and produce a hybrid that was permanently fertile. By this test man was a distinct species, but adaptable and plastic. (Dawson found additional support for this point in the abstracts of two papers published by the Linnaean Society in 1858 in which Alfred Russell Wallace and Charles Darwin each announced his discovery of evolution through natural selection.) Humanity had a common origin, but through migration and wide distribution in different zones of climate and food had come to differ considerably.

Both Dawson and Wilson were far more impressed by the capacities and characteristics common to all races, beside which colour, hair forms, or skull shapes seemed trivial. Dawson wrote of 'points of constancy' in all men, Wilson referred to 'instincts,' but both meant essentially the same qualities – an ability to acquire knowledge from experience and to communicate it and a capacity for a religious, spiritual feeling. Like other observers, they made much of affinities of language, especially in the Indo-European groups, as indicating common origins; like a number of other early, Canadian anthropologists, including Robert Grant Haliburton, they attached considerable significance to the occurrence of superstitions, festivals, and minor social customs in diverse peoples, for these also reinforced the belief in a single human community.[22] Their main emphasis, however, lay on the fact that everywhere human nature was essentially alike. This was not of course to say that all races were identical in achievement. Wilson, who dismissed the idea that a savage state necessarily indicated innate inferiority and could write of one American Indian language that it had 'grammatical forms as rich, regular, and consistent, as that in which Plato wrote, or Homer sung,' could still predict the ultimate disappearance of the native races of North America through absorption into the dominant European peoples.

The natural history of man, no less than geology or botany, was permeated by the same understanding of nature and expressed in virtually the same vocabulary. Nature was planned, orderly, harmonious, and benevolent. It cannot be emphasized too much that Nature was regarded as distinct from God; it was the handiwork of God, filled with clues and hints as to his intentions. (James Bovell wrote a long book for Canadian students warning them of the dangers of confusing the maker and works and lapsing into pantheism.)[23] Everything in nature worked just as it had been intended to function for the well-being of all things, and for man's instruction and benefit. The care with which the most insignificant animals were fitted for the places they occupied and the functions they performed implied that the creator could not be indifferent to a creature made in his own image.

It should be clear by now that natural theology was not so much about nature as about man's special place above and beyond nature. The whole of geological history seemed but a stupendous preparation for his arrival, and all of creation was arranged for him. Foresight had been shown in the laying down of coal measures, in the flow of the Gulf Stream that moderated the climate of western Europe in which His most blessed subjects lived, and even in arrangements in the insect world. How great should be our thankfulness, said the Reverend Charles Bethune in a discussion of parasites that preyed upon the Hessian fly and wheat midge, 'that the Almighty, in his wisdom, has created still more minute agents of His will to keep in check the work of destruction, and prevent the fair face of our land from soon becoming a desolate wilderness.'[24]

In Christian theology man was enjoined to use and subdue the earth and its creatures, convert it to a fit abode, and enjoy dominion from sea to sea. Man was God's steward on earth and charged with completing the creation. For Dawson – again it was he who made these matters most explicit – there was a single continuum stretching back to the remotest geological past and through scriptural history to the present and beyond. Man's relationship to the unfinished creation was at present abnormal because of the Fall, which for him was a historical as well as a moral fact, and the whole of nature was desolated and unsettled because of his tyranny. 'Man,' he wrote, 'is the capital of the column; and, if marred and defaced by moral evil, the symmetry of the whole is to be restored, ... by re-casting him in the image of his Divine Redeemer ... He has before him the option of being one with his maker, and sharing in a future glorious and finally renovated condition of our planet, or of sinking into endless degradation.'[25] The 're-casting' of man and his salvation would come through obedience to the laws of revelation, but in this science also was to play a part: it not only enlarged man's comprehension of God's will and intentions, but was also an instrument by which his creation would be turned into a 'renovated' estate. Thus science became an instrument of religious purposes.

From the claim that natural science was a way of learning about God, it followed that the practice of natural history was a singularly uplifting, moral discipline. In early Victorian Canada science was a novel enterprise, but it was not distinct from the prevailing religious and cultural temper. The naturalist, it was pointed out often enough, in studying nature was in effect retracing the thoughts of God and putting his mind in communion with the higher power as surely as if he were reading the words of scripture. Dawson, who laid the basis for McGill University's pre-eminence in Canadian science, and as principal could not disparage other branches of learning, none the less did feel that an individual who had mastered any department of nature had 'thereby acquired a mental training more god like in its character than any that can be gained from art or human literature, because he has been following in the footsteps, not of man, but of God.'[26]

A whole literature grew up extolling the subjective benefits to be derived from the pursuit of natural history and praising it as an especially useful way of employing leisure time. Boredom is an altogether neglected factor in intellectual history, but it was appreciated by those military officers and Hudson's Bay Company servants who recommended the study of nature as an antidote to the train of evils that followed from idleness and listlessness. In 1857, the *Canadian Naturalist and Geologist* reprinted an article by that English apostle of natural history, Charles Kingsley, who commended the study to the middle classes and held up the examples of a cultivated man, pent up all day in the drudgery of an office, who spent his evenings over a microscope and thus employed time that might otherwise have been wasted at the theatre; and of a London beauty who occupied her mind in a boudoir stocked with shells and fossils, flowers and seaweeds, and kept herself unspotted from the world. (Only much later would nature study be recommended as a remedy for female sexual self-abuse.)

The claim that natural history, by directing the mind from objects up to their creator, was a morally acceptable pastime or profession was made by naturalists as well as social moralists. 'Those interested in birds and flowers,' wrote the entomologist William Couper,' must be refined by the association. An intimate connection with the varied works of creation leads the mind from vicious associations, and preserves it from contact and con-tamination.' Science not only engaged and exercised the habits of accurate observation and systematic comparison, said Robert Bell, but it also trained the heart by bringing it into 'enlarged sympathy with the imminence of God. A true lover of nature cannot be a bad or selfish man.'[27]

Since nature stood for an overriding kindliness, its study was held to offer an unfailing source of consolation as well as plea-sure. Traill was a master at reminding her readers that nature never did betray the heart that loved her, and other apologists for natural history expanded upon the purely subjective grati-fications gained in its pursuit. Among these the enjoyment of beauty and the reassurance that the true lover of nature was never alone were always mentioned: much was made also of the enduring character of such pleasures. 'It appears to us,' wrote the botanist James Barnston, 'that it is only after a lapse of time, and especially when far removed from the scenes of botanical study, that we can appreciate its value.' Only he who had joined his friends in a botanical party and collected nature's treasures could understand that delight that sprung to the breast, not once, but also on many subsequent occasions, when a glance at a plant preserved in a herbarium awakened a happy memory of persons, places, and incidents. These sentiments that figured in justifications for natural history passed over into the experience of naturalists. John Macoun, not a sentimental man, could write with feeling of his 'sensations when I stand in a new field and see around me new forms and know that every step will add to my enjoyment. This brings up the days of yore when as a young man I tramped the woods alone, yet not alone for all around me were friends that reminded me of even earlier days when I, trowel in hand, but without knowledge dug up the primrose and violets for *my* garden in the far off time in Ireland.'[28]

It was indicative of the immensely practical spirit of colonial culture that even this claim, that the practice of natural history offered many emotional satisfactions, was hedged about by an emphasis upon the usefulness of pleasure itself. One stored the mind with such memories almost as an antidote to future tribulations and bereavements or took up a pastime that engaged and sharpened exactly those intellectual traits that were so necessary for success in business. The resonance of evangelical Protestantism and natural history lay deeper still. In a culture in which work was regarded as a moral discipline, and idleness was equated with sloth and hence guilt, recreation could not mean unprofitable relaxation. Every moment had to be filled with useful activity. It has been said that natural history in the Victorian period exercised a compelling fascination because 'it offered to the Evangelical character an unrivalled range of outlets for its expression.'[29] Diligent collecting, the piling up of facts, the measurement of work done in statistical terms of new species discovered or the size of collections all suggested a delight in industriousness and an earnestness that no doubt had their roots in science but were also fortified by religion.

In popular natural history the harmony and beneficence of nature were contrasted with the disharmony and maliciousness of human society. The early naturalists such as Gosse, and the founders of the societies who excluded contentious subjects from their meetings, spoke of the temple of science as a sanctuary removed from political and social discord. This exclusion of any topics that bore directly on social and economic relations may be construed as science turning away from society, but nothing could be further from the truth. The insistent repetition of the claim that science would foster commerce and agriculture had obvious social implications; so too, more subtly, did the constant emphasis upon the idea that 'a gradation of rank' existed throughout nature from the lowliest animal up to man, a point that left the unmistakable impression that the principles of the government in nature applied to human relations as well.[30] This idea was strengthened by the habit of writers of employing a political vocabulary, or words with political connotations, to describe the natural world as 'the Empire of nature,'[31] or comparing it to a well-run factory or workshop. By directing attention to things as they existed, indeed as they had been established by God, this science encouraged a conservatism with regard to social questions and underlined the beneficence of the prevailing order.

These underlying assumptions were made most explicit in the first half of the century and in the arguments of those who brought science to the mechanics' institutes, but it persisted throughout the Victorian period. The self-appointed tutors of the working class presented science as a road to self-improvement, morally as well as materially, and hoped that these bodies would further a closer conjunction of classes. Joseph Howe forthrightly told the Halifax Mechanics' Institute that service to science weaned the mind from the grosser propensities. When the organizers of the institute were criticized for encouraging the lower orders to aspire to advance beyond their appointed stations in life, they took some satisfaction in reporting that in the 1835 session the average attendance at the fifty two-hour lectures was one hundred and that thus ten thousand hours had 'been deducted from that portion of time which in this community would have been given up to dissipation.'[32] In this colonial town, with inhabitants so conscious of rank, not even a public appeal for a horticultural garden could avoid mentioning that it would be a wholesome alternative to the grog shops and, by bringing together the working man and his family with their better-dressed social superiors, would incite in them industry as well as sobriety. Whether expressly employed in such homilies as these, or simply held as an unstated assumption, the natural history of an ordered, ranked, supervised, and beneficent creation supported the fabric of Victorian society.

Naturalists, we should remind ourselves, were not primarily social commentators, still less theologians. They may have gone about their business oblivious to the philosophical ramifications of natural theology, only occasionally paying obeisance to its tenets. But far from being something extraneous to science, the idea of nature as the visible and tangible work of God permeated natural science, directing attention to what was fixed and above all to the marvellous adaptations in the natural world. And, coupled with the direct appeal to utility, it gave science a legitimacy in a profoundly religious culture. Naturalists, and not just theologians, insisted on this fusion of the sacred and the secular, and in this matter the Presbyterian Dawson was at one with the Catholic Provancher. It was precisely this identity of science and religion that was challenged and ultimately severed by Charles Darwin.

3

Nature

CHARLES DARWIN WAS the reluctant father of a revolution that ultimately destroyed traditional natural history and the amalgam of science and faith. With *The Origin of Species*, which he rushed into publication, under pressure of being anticipated, in 1859, Darwin made public a conviction that had grown in him for some twenty years. All living things, he had come to believe, had developed over a very long period from a single, primitive form of life. Despite the staggering detail and many illustrations that filled his book, the steps in Darwin's argument were stated with simplicity, precision, and great persuasive force. He argued that all forms of life possessed an inherent tendency to vary, a fact that man had employed for his own benefit in breeding domestic animals and birds and in cultivating plants. Since organisms multiplied at a faster rate than the available food supply and other means of support, there followed in nature an incessant competition and struggle for existence.

Those variations that gave individuals a competitive advantage in this struggle and enabled them to survive were preserved, transmitted to offspring, and consolidated in later generations until ultimately there developed forms essentially different from the originals. This preservation of favourable variations Darwin called natural selection, and natural selection, the key to his conception of evolution, he envisaged as having operated upon small differences, continuously, and incrementally. Species were thus made by nature, not by God. Darwin applied natural selection more explicitly to human origins in *The Descent of Man* (1871) and showed how man resembled the lower animals not only in physical characteristics but also in certain mental and emotional traits that had developed in the evolutionary process.

The idea of evolution through natural selection had repercussions upon every aspect of man's self-understanding. Because of the intimate association of natural history and religion in Britain, evolution inevitably brought into question the notion of the Bible as an inspired text in which God had spoken to man of his history, his duties, and his destiny. Evolution above all inverted the tenets of the old natural history tradition. For a benevolent, supervising deity it substituted a blind, relentless, physical process; for adaptations deliberately designed, random adjustments; for harmony, abiding violence and conflict; for plan and economy, order and balance, a chaotic wasteful process in which millions of beings were born only to die for no apparent purpose; for nature arranged for man's benefit, a natural law operating without any apparent regard for human values.

To juxtapose these points so sharply is to indicate the truly revolutionary character of Darwin's insight and to suggest also the painfulness of the adjustments he challenged Christian naturalists to make. But to put matters in this fashion also obscures the fact that the old natural theology had prepared the way for Darwin, by making familiar the idea of adaptation in nature, the progressive character of geological history, and the notion of God working through uniform natural law. 'If the Darwin theory is ever established,' Charles Lyell told William Dawson in 1860, 'it will be by the facts and arguments of the progressionists ... whose development doctrines go three parts of the way tho' they don't seem to see it.'[1] Naturalists working within the natural theology framework had accumulated the evidence by which that structure was destroyed.

The intense and extended debate over Darwin's evolution was not at bottom a conflict between religion and science, still less a battle between theologians and naturalists. In Britain and the United States leading Christian thinkers and many clergymen came to terms quite readily with evolution;[2] some scientists opposed Darwin and eventually accepted evolution while rejecting natural selection as its most important mechanism. Many scientists were also men of deep Christian commitment who found it inconceivable that God worked through such haphazard, brutal, and wasteful methods to produce the design of life. The essential controversy over Darwinianism was between those who wanted to retain theology within scientific explanation and those who believed that the notions of creation and providence had no place in natural history at all.

There was, moreover, nothing inevitable about the triumph of the Darwinian point of view, especially not in scientific circles. From the moment of its publication Darwin's hypothesis came under intense scrutiny and criticism which, in terms of the knowledge of the day, was reasonable and partly valid. Reviewers pointed to the statistical certainty that small variations in individuals would be swamped in cross-breeding; that the development of species from preceding forms found no confirmation in fossil history; that the entire theory rested on an unsatisfactory explanation of heredity and the transmission of parental characteristics; and that Darwin assumed a longer time frame for the operation of evolution than seemed reasonable to physicists who calculated the age of the earth on the basis of how long it had taken to cool to its present temperature. Some of these and additional points Darwin had anticipated; others caught him by surprise. In response he so modified his initial statement in the six editions of the *Origin* published between 1859 and 1872 that the theory became more complex if not muddled.[3]

Still, by the early 1870s, the majority of naturalists in Britain came to accept evolution as a legitimate and fruitful hypothesis, though they had great misgivings and reservations about the primacy that Darwin had given to natural selection. Judging by a survey of discussion in the British periodical press as the general acceptance of organic evolution grew, the repute of natural selection declined until what replaced Darwin's original formulation was a notion of predetermined evolution according to natural law, in which the deity did not continually intervene in his creation but had implanted in the first forms of life a capacity to develop progressively.[4] Other renditions of evolution were put forward by naturalists who called themselves allies of Darwin but whose ideas the master repudiated. The revolution in science that Darwin inaugurated was a long revolution. Some of the elements most essential to its support were discovered only after the end of the Victorian century. It is necessary to emphasize the uncertainty and confusion surrounding Darwin's theory as a preliminary to considering the responses of Canadian naturalists, because our present knowledge makes the outcome seem inexorable and tempts us to dismiss his critics as obscurantists.

The initial reactions to Darwin's book among the few academic naturalists in Canada hardly differed from the more critical responses in Britain and the United States.[5] William Dawson, in the *Canadian Naturalist*, and Daniel Wilson and the University College (Toronto) geologist Edward J. Chapman, in the *Canadian Journal*, were filled with admiration for the care and patience with which he had marshalled an immense array of factual material, but they were sceptical about his main conclusion. By insisting that Darwin had not accounted for the origin of life but only advanced a theoretical explanation for derivation, they reduced the issue to a secondary question. On this level the issue was not whether species varied but by how much. Both Darwin and Wilson were quite receptive to Darwin's abundantly documented point that species varied enormously, because this strengthened their own case against the advocates of the multiple creation of man. If, as Darwin had showed, domestic pigeons descended from a common type differed in so many features, then it seemed much more likely that the human races of Europe, Africa, and America were also all descended from a common stock. But that varieties had through natural selection developed into distinct species they could not accept.

On this point geological history spoke with conclusive authority. That history was crucial for Darwin's case, for it alone supplied positive evidence of unlimited variation in the succession of animal and plant life and of the transitions from one species to another. This argument is exactly what palaeontology did not support,[6] and Darwin had explained away this discrepancy by claiming that the fossil record was incomplete and fragmentary and would remain so, since the conditions conducive to the emergence of new types were unfavourable for the preservation of fossils.

For Dawson, geology became the major battlefield of evolutionary theory, and he was strongest here, where Darwin seemed to be weakest. It could be reasonably claimed not only that Darwin had exaggerated the imperfections of that history, but that, more positively, the sequence of development confirmed the fixity of major types over millions of years. Drawing upon his own research, Dawson was able to claim that a comparison of shells from post-Pliocene deposits with those then living in the Gulf of St Lawrence showed no evolutionary change; similarly he was to point out that his findings in the Devonian and Silurian flora confirmed the same truth.

In his later works Dawson presented a reading of the fossil series that emphasized that animals and plants first appeared not in embryonic, primitive forms, but highly developed and specialized; the very oldest rocks contained fossils of a multitude of beings, all distinct, with remarkably developed anatomies and perfect eyes. New types appeared that had no apparent predecessors, others vanished without successors. There was no continuous chain of succession containing intermediate forms and connecting links. The pattern of the appearance of life in the past resembled the undulations of great waves, with sudden and rapid influxes of new forms that showed a considerable tendency to vary at first and gradually tapered off to extinction. This general pattern was still progressive, but it was characterized by dramatic breaks, discontinuity, and the abrupt appearance of generic types.[7]

Not only did the geological record stand in refutation of slow, continuous transformation of species, but also it offered little evidence of natural selection in the struggle for existence. Competition and struggle, far from being the chief cause of development, could and did lead to degeneration and extinction. Dawson could not bring himself to accept the new view of nature upon which Darwin's evolutionary synthesis was based, and though he admitted that the struggle between overpopulation and limited food supply might affect individual species he continued to think of nature as essentially harmonious in the sense that there was always sufficient food and living space.

Darwinian evolution was condemned also for violating accepted scientific procedure. Darwin's argument was hypothetical: he advanced and illustrated certain general statements and assumptions and upon these built a logical case for evolution. Natural selection was set out as the most probable explanation of the known facts of natural history rather than as a confirmed and demonstrated truth. To a large extent his whole argument rested on the analogy between domestic breeding and selection in nature – a false analogy, claimed one critic, because domestication was successful precisely because animals were isolated from nature and, when returned to the wild, reverted to their original forms.[8] When these critics objected to what they called Darwin's bold speculations, unproven inferences, and mistaken analogies, they were defending a mode of scientific inquiry that concentrated upon the painstaking accumulation of facts. If, as Darwin claimed, the fossil record was incomplete, then it seemed to them that scientific effort must continue the search for the missing material, suspend generalization, and not attempt impatiently to surmount such difficulties with fanciful theories. Between Darwin's method and Dawson's critique of it there yawned a gulf that indicated the distance between the old natural history and the new biology. Dawson was essentially upholding a method of scientific investigation by which he had gained his reputation and to which the natural history societies were devoted. Repeatedly, he reminded the members of the Natural History Society of Montreal that they had a broader and richer field for scientific work than the naturalists of the Old World and that their true course lay in 'patient, honest, and careful accumulation of facts,' not in emulation of the metropolitan intellectuals in 'building up specious fabrics of conjecture.'[9]

This dispute over scientific procedure quickly revealed itself as a clash of opinion over the limits of science itself. Before Darwin, naturalists had by and large associated the mystery of mysteries – the appearance of new species – with supernatural causes. Creation meant the direct intervention of God in nature by whatever means, to make something new. Creation always defined the point beyond which scientific explanation could not go.[10] Darwin had hesitantly come to the view that this way of thinking impeded scientific understanding, became a substitute for explanation, and should be dispensed with entirely. In the *Origin*, Darwin applied to biology the same type of reasoning that Lyell had employed to account for the history of the earth: scientific interpretation had to do exclusively with material forces and regularities that were observable, verifiable, and not subject to unpredictable intervention. Darwin's most revolutionary step was to extricate scientific explanation from the religious matrix in which it had been nurtured and to try to drive out of science any religious points of reference.

Darwin's Canadian critics either explicitly recognized or vaguely sensed that with the theory of evolution science had somehow transgressed its proper limits and was claiming to explain a reality that was both material and spiritual on materialist grounds alone. Referring to the strange resemblances between animals and the remarkable fact that some were equipped with rudimentary organs of no apparent use to them but useful to other related forms, Edward Chapman could say only that these things he regarded as part of a great plan 'for some purpose unfathomable to us at present, and perhaps ever to remain unfathomable to our restricted power of enquiry. Beyond this, they are inexplicable to us, as the object of our presence here is inexplicable.'[11] Dawson was quite emphatic in saying that Darwin and his supporters had been so intoxicated by the genuine achievements of Victorian science that they seemed to believe that science could account for all problems of life and nature. To begin by excluding any notion of final cause and then to construct arguments confined to material forces was to argue, to no purpose, in a circle. 'Even when it professes to admit the existence of God,' Dawson wrote, 'the evolutionist reasoning of our day contents itself altogether with the physical or visible universe, and leaves entirely out of sight the powers of the unseen and the spiritual.' Science had necessarily to be limited on all sides by a sense of mystery: to Dawson it seemed that the origin of species might be one of those ultimate facts beyond which science by its own legitimate methods could not penetrate.[12]

In the early 1860s it seemed reasonable to suppose that the theory of natural selection was but a momentary craze and that it would soon follow into obscurity earlier theories of transmutation that had been discredited. Dawson had lived through intense controversies in geology that had involved the statements of extreme and mutually exclusive positions only to see them modified, qualified, and integrated into a synthesis that was quite compatible with scripture. It was understandable that he expected that Darwin too would have a similar future: he would be remembered for the way he had expanded man's understanding of the extent of variation, while his more extravagant analogies and speculations would be put aside. But by the early 1870s naturalists in Britain and the United States, whatever their reservations about natural selection, had by and large accepted evolution. And even worse, this triumph of evolution encouraged the most extensive applications of materialist interpretations to man's origins and his place in nature.

Dawson threw himself into a defence of the traditional natural history with a zeal that was obsessive and found few, if any, parallels among naturalists elsewhere. In his presidential addresses to the Natural History Society of Montreal, in many speeches to religious assemblies and theological colleges, and in a series of books (some sponsored by the Religious Tract Society) intended for the educated lay reader, he campaigned against the evolutionists tenaciously and relentlessly. With *Story of the Earth and Man* (1873), *Origin of the World* (1877), and *Modern Ideas of Evolution* (1890), Dawson gained a reputation as 'the most distinguished anti-Darwinian in the English-speaking world,'[13] and also as a discerning critic who not only carefully separated Darwin's from other theories of mutation, but also kept fully abreast of the flood of literature on the subject. The essential views that he had expressed in *Archaia* in 1860 he found little reason to change in 1877, or for that matter in 1890, though he assimilated into his argument and used for his own purposes new viewpoints on natural selection proposed by its European critics and travelled a considerable distance from his earliest views regarding the immutability of species to recognize capacities of variation and change under law. Yet in the end Dawson simply could not move beyond a belief in creation. By creation, he explained, he did not mean miraculous intervention: the creation of species took place by 'the continuous introduction of new forms of life under definite laws, but by a power not emanating from within themselves, nor from the inanimate nature surrounding them.'[14]

Dawson's long campaign against Darwin was expressive of more than opposition on scientific grounds, more even than his inability to accept the exclusion of religion from science. Into his later books and essays there crept a certain hysteria regarding the social and moral implications of evolution and a sense of embattlement with threatening forces. The single most horrifying point of evolution to Dawson was its direct bearing on human origins. Darwin had shifted the entire debate about man from the unity of the human species to a consideration of man's descent from ape-like ancestors. That man had also derived through natural and sexual selection and that his intellectual and spiritual qualities and even moral sense may have been accidental by-products of a struggle for existence were ideas from which Dawson recoiled with loathing and disgust. The survival of the fittest as applied to man, he wrote, 'is nothing less than the basest and most horrible superstition. It makes man not merely carnal, but devilish. It takes his lowest appetites and propensities, and makes them his God and creator.'[15]

Scarcely less serious, he charged, the very propagation by scientific thinkers of the notion of God removed from nature and of struggle, competition, and survival of the fittest was itself bound to weaken and diminish religious belief and ultimately have destructive effects on the whole structure of society. Personal and social morality had been founded on the simple belief in future rewards and punishments: the removal of a superintending deity from nature was bound to shake this faith. The old natural history may have had only an indirect and remote connection with any explicit political or social teaching, but back of the insistence upon a ruling providence in nature lay the clear implication that 'if God's role as an immediate, if occasional adjuster of the material world was whittled away, He would also be displaced as a governor of its inhabitants.'[16] A Darwinian universe of no evident design, of only senseless accident, was for Dawson quite literally the enthronement of unreason and would inevitably lead to the brutalization of human relations. The subsequent application of the struggle of existence and the survival of the fittest to social, class, and race relations filled him with the same dread that had darkened Darwin's last years.

Dawson's stature as a scientist and his position as an educational leader in Canadian society were no less bound up with his resistance to evolution. Though he posed as a mediator between legitimate scientific knowledge and unwarranted speculation, Dawson at times seemed possessed by the spirit of the combative sectarian. In 1860 he assessed Darwin's book in an even-handed manner; by 1872 he was attacking the men who supported this unproven dogma and were able to disseminate their opinions in the London journals. Increasingly isolated from the British scientific establishment, relying for gossip upon older men – such as the geologist J.J. Bigsby – who had become outsiders, Dawson himself became a victim of the politics of the Darwinian revolution.

In 1870 Dawson prepared for the Royal Society of London the prestigious Bakerian lecture on the pre-Carboniferous flora of North America upon which he had laboured for some twenty years; the publications committee of the society thought his concluding remarks on the persistence of basic types inappropriate and for this and probably other reasons recommended against its publication.[17] If there is anything more calculated to inflame the anger of an academic than such criticism of a paper, it is being turned down for a research grant. Dawson suffered this indignity too. In 1877 he had sufficiently subdued his prejudices against the Royal Society to apply for a small grant in aid of his continuing exploration for the remains of land animals in the Nova Scotia coal-beds. He was not successful.[18]

These rebuffs from men at the centre of imperial science could not help but intensify the vehemence of Dawson's assaults on Darwin's supporters as 'scientific banditti' anxious to further their own careers by embracing fashionable theories irrespective of their intrinsic scientific merits.[19] Throughout Dawson's commentary on the reasons why evolution was so widely accepted by British men of science there runs a feeling that the metropolitan intellectuals had been carried away and that the true Baconian mission of science was somehow to be represented by the natural history societies in Canada. This was not the last time that a Canadian would instruct the imperial centre on its proper duties.

Dawson's opposition to the Darwinian party cannot be explained away on grounds of self-interest, but self-interest did fortify the relentlessness of his war against doctrines of materialistic evolution. His own view of himself as an inhabitant of a beleaguered outpost was a product not only of his status as the last major geologist who was not an evolutionist but also of his position as a defender of the interests of the Anglo-Protestant minority in Quebec in the midst of the ultramontanist campaign against science and for the elevation of the Catholic church in all spheres of life. When he turned down an attractive offer of a position at Princeton in 1878 he made very explicit the worries that lay back of his obsessions:

The claims of duty tie me to this place while an important handful of protestant people are holding an advanced front in the midst of Ultramontanism, and where, but for the utmost efforts of all willing to help, the cause of liberal education and science as well as religion is likely to be overwhelmed, and with it all reasonable chance of the permanent success of our Canadian Dominion, for unless the gospel and the light of Modern civilization can overcome popery in French Canada our whole system will break up. Further we have here also those beginnings of materialism which are threatening you, and it seems impossible to desert the friends who have fought with me more or less successfully in the past 20 years in the double-handed fight.[20]

The truth might need repeating many times lest it be lost sight of, but Dawson's prolonged campaign for science (true science, that is) was clearly linked to his solicitude for the minority that was its main support.

It is ironical that one of the forces within Quebec society that stimulated Dawson's alarm may also have intensified the dilemma of French Canada's leading naturalist. Abbé Provancher was devoted to the popularization of natural science among French Canadians at a time when one party among the clerical leaders of that province was condemning liberalism and materialistic science as enemies of both religion and national survival. The regard for science in French-Canadian culture had been weak, science was associated with the alien English-Canadian ascendancy, and it may well be that the ultramontanist onslaught upon modernity turned a pre-existing indifference into a hostility.

Provancher faced the same dilemma in science that the young Wilfrid Laurier confronted in politics. Just as Laurier tried to establish a basis for a liberalism stripped of its anti-clerical and revolutionary associations, so too Provancher attempted to divest natural science of the materialism that had been censured in papal encyclicals. He did so by restating the essential tenets of the natural theology tradition in terms and analogies that hardly differed from those of Gosse, Traill, or Dawson.

Provancher confronted *le Darwinisme* directly in a dozen articles published in his journal between January 1887 and March 1888. Setting out to show the absurdity of evolution, he used scientific objections that were by then commonplace. But his case on scientific grounds was very general and based on two popular accounts: he referred only once to the existence of a French edition of Darwin's *Origin*, a book that he apparently did not own,[21] mentioned none of the classics of natural history on this question, and, unlike Dawson, hardly referred to those fields – botany and entomology – in which he was knowledgeable as offering evidence one way or another. For Provancher the scientific case against evolution was clearly secondary to the religious and social reasons for rejecting an impious doctrine that removed God from nature, brought the authenticity of miracles, including creation, into question, and made man the descendant of beasts. Provancher and Dawson totally agreed on this fundamental matter, but Dawson's case against evolution, far more than Provancher's, was set within the broad context of the scientific debate and drew upon the total range of the international literature. Provancher's discussion accorded priority to religion.

So too, in its own way, did Daniel Wilson's. When Darwin's book appeared in 1859 Wilson was putting the finishing touches on *Prehistoric Man: Researches into the Origin of Civilisation in the Old and the New World* (1862), in which he defined 'man's innate capacity,' through a comparison of the cultures of early Europe with those of the Americas, past and present. A work of immense erudition, filled with an astonishing array of information – on metallurgy and technology, religious rites and buildings, languages and superstitions – these two plump volumes were intended to confirm and illustrate one central point: that man everywhere and at all times had revealed an instinctive ingenuity in invention and in artistic and religious expression. All men, from the rudest 'savages' to the 'civilized' Victorians, possessed distinctive attributes that decisively separated them from animals – notably intelligence and the capacity for advancing from their past states, or relapsing into them, under the most diverse conditions imaginable.

Inevitably Wilson read Darwin with these preoccupations uppermost in his mind. A more resilient critic than Dawson, better informed about the contemporary literature on the natural history of man, Wilson found the evidence that man had been on earth for more than a few thousand years irresistible, and in time he accepted a good deal of the evolutionists' case. 'We are ready with the admission,' he wrote, somewhat reluctantly, in 1873,

That all life starts from a cell; that the primary rule of embryonic development is to all appearances common to animal life; that the human embryo in early stages is not readily discernible from that of inferior animals very remote from man; and recognize the whole very remarkable homologous structure in man and the lower animals ... But what we have to complain of in the treatment of a question involving such far-reaching results is that the modern evolutionist, leading us on clearly, and on the whole convincingly ... and recognizing in so far the essential element of humanity as to push researches beyond mere physical structure in search of intellect, the social virtues, and a moral sense: just at the final stage where the wondrous transformation is to be looked for on which the verdict depends, we are directed solely to physical evidence, as though brain, reason, mind, and soul, were convertible terms.[22]

Like Alfred Russell Wallace, the co-discoverer of natural selection, Wilson could not imagine how man's intellectual capacity had been evolved out of material nature.

This hesitation before the great question might be attributed to Wilson's religious faith; but he insisted that the evolutionists' conviction that there must be some missing link between the higher apes and man, or between the repetitive mechanical instincts in animals and the creative intelligence of man, was also a matter of faith.

It was typical of Wilson, a cultured man of letters as well as an ethnologist, that he should register his opposition to evolution as applied to man in a literary study of Caliban from Shakespeare's *The Tempest*. In claiming that this imaginary creature – a transitional form between the true brute and a human being – was a more convincing 'missing link' than anything conjured up by the followers of Darwin, Wilson was up to more than indulging in a whimsical, scholarly joke. For he proceeded to show how Shakespeare had created Caliban out of the common beliefs of his age – in monsters, giants, and supernatural creatures. The nineteenth century, like the sixteenth, had encountered unknown and unexplored worlds, and the missing links invented by the Victorian scientist were as imaginative as those strange approximations to humanity that were reported by his predecessors to inhabit the newly discovered continents. These days, as before, Wilson said, science makes its own gnomes and naiads.

By neither training nor temperament was Wilson in any position to challenge the theory of natural selection on technical grounds: what he did object to was the unrestrained temptation to add up physical resemblances and assume that these implied mental and emotional continuities as well. If he tried to show how modern science had become excessively speculative and arrogant in its materialism, he was equally emphatic in condemning the distrust of science generally in some religious circles. The 'progress of scientific truth,' he declared publicly more than once, 'has been hindered by theological restraint; and some of the grandest revelations of science have not only been received with suspicion, but have been denounced as in conflict with religion.'[23]

As a teacher at University College and after 1880 its principal, Wilson was a consistent supporter of the non-denominational, secular university, in large part because he believed that science could be most effectively taught and practised in an institutional setting free of the prospects of clerical intervention. And, not unlike Dawson and Provancher, he experienced the predicament of being caught between clashes of 'religion' (with its sectarian passions and mistrust of all science) and 'science' (with its extravagant claims). On one occasion, in March 1887, a few days before Alfred Russell Wallace was to speak at University College, Wilson fretted that the title of his first lecture – 'Darwinism' – was 'enough to bring the clergy down on us in full-force, for the very name of Darwin is to most of them like a red rag to a bull; and the greater their ignorance the more pronounced their dogmatism.' True enough, there were long letters in the press and one to Wilson from a graduate protesting the use of Convocation Hall to spread atheism. At another time Wilson was questioned by a student about a statement that appeared in a joint publication regarding the antiquity of man. On following up the matter, he discovered that a comment by the English anthropologist E.B. Tylor had been inserted into his own work, and he reflected: 'I shall not be surprised to find the 'Dominion Churchman' or the 'Christian Guardian' down on me for some of Tylor's free talk. Men may venture on sayings in the orthodox precincts of Oxford that dare not be whispered in the State University of Ontario.'[24]

This constant possibility of misunderstanding may have made Wilson cautious and tentative in public, but in private he was less inhibited about expressing his anxieties. After reading Darwin's life and letters, he told Dawson he was struck at how the great naturalist gradually ceased being able to see truth in anything that he could not see or touch. 'The ultimate agnostic's creed,' he commented, 'and his passing into the great darkness, as though life were but a lamp, enkindled and going out, when its oil failed; with no replenishing, seemingly no hope of a hereafter; left on my own mind a shuddering sense of pain. The separation from our loved ones,' Wilson added (this three years after his wife's passing), 'would be terrible indeed, if we could think that death meant such annihilation.'[25] For this first generation of naturalists to confront Darwin, this 'shuddering sense of pain' was at least as much a cause for rejecting evolution as were any of the scientific arguments, persuasive as some of these were.

In the history of the accommodation that Canadian naturalists made with Darwin, Dawson was an untypical, not a representative figure. In contrast to him, with his single-minded, militant campaign, most naturalists in the last four decades of the century maintained a puzzling reticence on the idea of evolution. After the flurry of reviews of the 1860s, they seldom wrote general appraisals of the theory and kept to themselves whatever spiritual anguish this new view of life may have caused them. They did not compete with literary men and philosophers who filled the pages of the quarterlies with articles on the unsettling effects of science on morality and philosophy. They may have abdicated the responsibility that their special knowledge placed upon them of mediating and interpreting science to the public, though any literate Canadian could draw freely from the abundance of such popular literature from Britain or the United States.

In the transactions of the natural history societies the first principles of evolution were rarely discussed, except in Montreal where Dawson kept the issue in the foreground. In their memoirs, individual naturalists were on this subject laconic to the point of being unhelpful. William Logan, whose caution and circumspection might have been reinforced by his delicate position as a state employee, always avoided discussing subjects that touched upon religion.[26] The Presbyterian and self-taught botanist John Macoun merely referred to his reading of Hugh Miller and to the congruence between geology and the six periods of creation and added: 'Since then I never doubted the authenticity of the Bible ... After this time I could never see how a naturalist could doubt the existence of God.'[27] University of New Brunswick geologist Loring Woart Bailey seemed outwardly untroubled by the controversy, managed to give advice on these scientific matters to laymen and clergy alike, and wrote an elementary text for schools in 1887 that praised the plan and the manifestations of divine wisdom in nature.[28]

Such affirmations of tradition were not disingenuous: some naturalists were men of deep religious feeling who were as offended by the materialism of evolution as Dawson or any Christian minister. Henry Youle Hind, the explorer-geologist, wrote a negative review of Lyell's *Antiquity of Man* (1863), which challenged the short period in the biblical chronology and leaned towards the theory of natural selection; Hind said that if scientific facts contradicted scripture then men must inquire into the sources of human error. James Fletcher, a lay reader in the Anglican church, told Catherine Parr Traill in 1883 how attractive he found her manuscript on plants 'after the irreverent materialistic philosophy, falsely so called, of too many of our modern naturalists. It is very charming to me to see such love for our beneficent creator and reverence for his perfect works. In all my instructions in botany I have always endeavoured to draw attention to the marvelous and beautiful adaptations of all objects presented to us in the study of nature.'[29]

The reception of Darwin in Canadian scientific circles was initially critical and remained restrained and muted. Not only did the country produce no fervent champions of evolution to challenge the overwhelming dominance of idealism in the educated élite, but also scientific journals preserved a puzzling reticence on the general theory. Canadian naturalists were reluctant to be drawn into theoretical discussion because Darwin's hypothetical mode of argument was so alien to the tradition in which they had been trained and also because his theory did not impinge directly upon the collecting and classifying activities in which most of them were engaged. It was not necessary for, say, Macoun to resolve for himself the many disputed aspects of evolution in order to proceed with his explorations and inventory.

This reticence regarding evolution may have been reinforced by the fact that in Canada science was in the process of establishing its own legitimacy. Throughout the century scientists showed an acute sensitivity to what they saw as a lingering prejudice against such inquiry on religious grounds. As early as 1830 the leaders of the Natural History Society of Montreal were accused of promoting atheism because science distracted the mind of the student 'from having the Almighty continuously in view.' A soldier-geologist told Logan in 1856 that he had attempted to reconcile the Mosaic record with geological facts 'as an answer to an attack made by certain persons who considered themselves more religious than their neighbours and therefore deemed a supporter of Geology must perforce be an Infidel.' Much later Thomas Weston, another geologist, encountered a similar response from a rural couple in New Brunswick who watched him chisel a fossil fish from a rock, and, when told that it was millions of years old, enjoined him to leave alone the stone fish that God had placed there and said prayers for his misguided soul. In 1883 A.H. MacKay wrote of the diminution – not the disappearance – of 'the lurking suspicion that has crept down through the centuries from the dark ages, that science is in some mysterious manner connected with the powers of darkness.'[30] The answer to all such perceived suspicions was the tradition of natural theology. It is not necessary to doubt that naturalists believed in the idea that the study of nature enhanced the understanding of God to see that this claim also forestalled or neutralized charges of impiety.

When the storm over Darwin's book first broke the few naturalists in colleges had been appointed very recently and the natural history societies were only beginning to emerge. Naturalists were actively furthering a greater public awareness and recognition of science at a time when science itself was being compromised by the widely publicized pronouncements of the more extreme British evolutionists. The advocates of natural history would not have been aiding its cause had they indulged in debates about the origin of species with all the metaphysical problems this would have inevitably raised. They continued to invoke the congenial associations of science and religion throughout the late nineteenth century.

The idea of evolution made its way in Canada not through noisy debate over abstract theory but by subtle penetration into the practice and writing of natural history. It is evident that the army surgeon Leith Adams had been alerted by Darwin to paying attention to the ways that a cold climate affected bird life and especially to fixing upon any deviations from established habits in creatures, for these, he said, pointed 'towards the solution of important questions pertaining to the origin of species.'[31] When Darwin's name figured in the publications of the natural history societies and especially in the transactions of the Royal Society, it was most often with reference to the bearings of his insights upon concrete problems of research. The Royal Society in 1887, for example, published several papers that illustrate this process clearly.

In one the botanist George Lawson, who had earlier dismissed natural selection applied to plant life, dealt rather tentatively with the origin and distribution of the Arctic flora. He took as his point of departure Darwin's observation that the northern plants were of a great antiquity, had been driven southward in the glacial period, and, with the succeeding warmth, had spread northward, bringing with them species from the zones they had invaded and leaving behind stragglers on the mountains in warmer areas. Any consideration of this claim, Lawson noted, necessarily involved consideration of variation, adaptation, and survival as well as a comparison of the Arctic flora of Canada with that of northern Europe. Such an approach was quite different from the view that plants were independent creations specially fitted for the places in which they were found.[32]

Another paper, by the McGill physiologist Wesley Mills, had to be prepared tactfully in order to ensure it an unprejudiced hearing: the topic was 'Squirrels: Their Habits and Intelligence, with Special Reference to Feigning.' Darwin had underscored an essential kinship between animals and men, in intellectual as well as physical descent, and argued that the differences in the mental behaviour and capacities of the two were differences of degree, not of kind. It seemed to him likely that man's self-conscious reasoning, even his moral sentiments, were extensions of the mental endowments of creatures below him in nature. Anti-evolutionists always insisted that the gulf between the mechanical and repetitive character of the behaviour of animals and man's ability to reach abstract knowledge and express himself in speech was as wide and distinct as the gap separating species. But for Mills and others more responsive to Darwin, the continuity of mental operations of animals and man provided an exciting incentive to the observation of animal behaviour and imparted to an old subject a new objective and enhanced importance.

Mills laid out the basis of enquiry in strict Darwinian terms: 'If we regard man as the outcome of development through lower forms, according to variation with natural selection, – in a word, if a man is the final link in a long chain binding the whole animal creation together, we have the greater reason for inferring that comparative psychology and human psychology have common roots. We must, in fact, believe in a mental or psychic evolution as well as in a physical (morphological) one.'[33] Thus it became important to understand the behaviour of animals, their reasoning power, the ways they communicate, and their capacity to learn. Was the habit of squirrels to feign death or injury blind and unreflective instinct, deliberate behaviour learned from experience, or physical paralysis produced by fear? And could this activity be explained in terms of natural selection?

In this and other papers of the 1880s and 1890s, collected in *The Nature and Development of Animal Intelligence* (1898), Mills was continually impressed by the plasticity of living things and by the various ways in which animal instincts seemed modified by experience, even though he could not demonstrate that individual animals who sometimes went beyond the stage of intelligence attained by the mass of their species passed on this advantage to their offspring.

By a similar route from Darwin, Ernest Thompson Seton also came to reject animal instinct as fixed, but he pursued the subject beyond the boundaries of orthodox natural history when, in his many animal stories, he tried to penetrate into the minds of individual animals and describe their feelings and motives. That this study of animal behaviour ended in fiction and sentimentalism should not, however, obscure the fact that this most respectable field of inquiry rested in part on Darwinian premises.

Darwin's ideas were also diffused by teachers and popularizers who may not have accepted all elements of the theory of evolution but who still found that the hypothesis enabled naturalists to make sense of relationships formerly unintelligible. The principal of the Pictou Academy, Alexander MacKay, explained and justified the new system of classification on such grounds. The artificial system of Linnaeus, he wrote in 1883, had grouped plants in terms of a single outstanding characteristic; the natural system that replaced it in the course of the nineteenth century was based on general structures and natural relationships. 'A family of plants ... according to the hypothesis of modern evolution,' he explained, 'would indicate a group of species which might have been descended from some single plant long ages ago. By such unaccountable changes as we see take place to a small extent in the cultivation of plants to-day, it is supposed that in the course of ages, by a wide distribution, under diverse climatic conditions, plants changed their forms ... Perhaps, then, all plants were ultimately derived from some one original form. Such an hypothesis,' he continued, 'is of course very difficult of proof; but as it forms a very convenient and natural basis of classification, which is not positively negatived by any known fact, it is therefore at least a good working hypothesis to enable us to arrange our knowledge and ultimately discover new facts.' On the validity of the theory of evolution as a whole, MacKay suspended judgment: he supported the hypothesis on the more limited grounds that it made more sense of the patterns and relations in botany. Ramsay Wright, who taught natural history at the University of Toronto, was less reserved: in a text published in 1889 and authorized for the new high school course in zoology, Wright presented organic evolution as the principle integrating the whole field.[34]

Aspects of evolution entered into the thinking and practice of Canadian naturalists in a pre-eminently Darwinian way – slowly and selectively. Like men of science elsewhere, these Canadians were quite familiar with all the difficulties with the general theory and aware of how Darwin's initial generalizations changed – and continued to be changed by others – in the last third of the century. They knew, as some publicists all too obviously did not, that the status of natural selection was quite problematic and that acceptance of evolution involved much more than a declaration of faith in an assumption. Still, even those with reasonable reservations readily agreed that the hypothesis had already revolutionized the study of natural history and was the best starting point in the subject.[35] Because the progress of Darwinism was so protracted it is impossible to date with precision when the majority of Canadian naturalists accepted some form of evolution. It has been argued that in Australia acceptance of evolution by scientists occurred in the mid-1890s and even then mainly in university departments of biology and physiology. In Canada the most confident announcements that all problems with evolution had been cleared away came from university biologists after the turn of the century.[36]

The gradual triumph of the Darwinian point of view was marked by the steady disappearance of references to creation or God in nature from the literature of science and the gradual acceptance that the parting between science and religion was no longer a temporary separation but a permanent divorce. When William Dawson died in 1899 two geologists of another generation surveyed his contribution to science: Frank Adams dismissed his books on the agreement between science and scripture as having once met a popular need and comforted many pious souls, but predicted – quite wrongly – that these were not the works by which he would be remembered; Henry Ami judged these exercises as having played a part in establishing the accepted equilibrium between science and religion as 'two separate spheres.'[37] It was exactly this contention that Dawson had battled against all his life, and it was precisely here that Darwin's long revolution in science won out most decisively.

For natural history Darwin's legacy was ambiguous. Evolution enhanced the status of the natural sciences and gave them an integrating principle. It also, however, ultimately reinforced tendencies towards specialization that were leading to the disintegration of the old natural history. Natural history was primarily descriptive and observational, concerned with the form, structure, and adaptation of whole organisms and with their role in the economy of nature. The naturalist rejoiced in field study and in the direct observation of living things and had coupled accuracy of description with the aesthetic and emotional appreciation of nature. In the post-Darwin period, biology – the study of living organisms – was transformed by the principle of evolution and came to focus upon problems of the origin, derivation, and function of organs. The new investigators left the field for the laboratory, probed beneath the surface of things and set out to discover how particular adaptations had come to be. The day was past, E.W. MacBride, the new professor of zoology at McGill, announced to the Natural History Society of Montreal in 1899, 'when a natural history society could be held to justify its existence by the mere collecting and naming of species ... Once the local fauna is fairly well known, the object of the naturalist is to study each species in relation to its environment, and leaving to the anatomist the task of elucidating the past history and wider relationships of an animal from its internal structure, to determine what effect its present surroundings have on it; in a word, to study evolution in action.'[38]

The study of evolution in action was beyond the resources of the societies, and after the turn of the century there grew within these circles the realization that their period of vitality was over, that science had become intensely specialized and discovery more difficult, and that the day of the now old-fashioned all-round naturalist had passed. These societies had been displaced by universities and government agencies, and they increasingly turned to the promotion of popular education, especially nature study in the schools, and conservation. After 1900 it was possible – it still is – for part-time naturalists to record important observations, but within science, even in Canada, natural history had been relegated to the sidelines.

The decline of natural history was registered above all by the fragmentation of that Victorian amalgam of science and religion, of fact and feeling, and of that sense of intellectual progress and popular participation. Natural history had reflected and channelled some of the strongest drives in colonial culture. It was an instrument for the appropriation and control of nature and a vehicle through which divine purpose stood revealed; it was at once an acceptable form of leisure and a path to recognition; it provided an outlet for intellectual activity in a colonial environment that seemed to have no past and no traditions to stimulate the literary imagination.

Natural history left its mark not only in the creation of Canada's scientific institutions but also in the early poetry of Archibald Lampman, the animal stories of Charles G.D. Roberts and Ernest Thompson Seton, and the nature essays of S.T. Wood. And it lived on in the feelings of such representative Victorians as Sir Wilfrid Laurier and Sir Robert Borden, who found pleasure in this appreciation of nature. So vividly could Laurier recall the birds around the Arthabaskaville of his youth – their plumage, songs, nests, colours, and numbers of eggs – and so convincingly could he explain why some species disappeared and others replaced them, that the hard-boiled politician Charlie Murphy thought he might have been a professor of ornithology. Borden, who never learned the names of half the members of his Unionist caucus, knew the botanical names of all the Canadian wild flowers that he cultivated in his garden.

This feeling for natural history also entered into the experiences of younger men who were to help reshape Canadian intellectual life in the twentieth century. It was evident in Harold Innis, whose study of the fur trade began with an extended chapter on the life history of the beaver; in Arthur Lower, who collected plants and insects in his youth, and whose love of nature helped turn him to an examination of the forest as a factor in the shaping of Canadian experience; in the German-born Frederick Philip Grove, who enriched Canadian literature with two little classics in the naturalist tradition, *Over Prairie Trails* (1922) and *The Turn of the Year* (1923). These examples not only confirm the prominent place of natural history in the imagination of Victorians but also indicate the endurance of its legacy long after the Victorian century had closed.

Notes

ABBREVIATIONS

BA *The British American Magazine devoted to Literature, Science and Art*
CJ *Canadian Journal of Industry, Science and Art*
CNG *Canadian Naturalist and Geologist*
CNQJS *Canadian Naturalist and Quarterly Journal of Science*
CRS *Canadian Record of Science*
MU McGill University, Montreal
NC *Le Naturaliste canadien*
NHSNB *Bulletin, Natural History Society of New Brunswick*
NSINS *Proceedings, Nova Scotia Institute of Natural Science* (after 1894,
 Proceedings, the Nova Scotian Institute of Science)
ON *The Ottawa Naturalist*
OFNC *Transactions, Ottawa Field Naturalists' Club*
PAC Public Archives of Canada, Ottawa
PANS Public Archives of Nova Scotia, Halifax
LHSQ *Transactions of the Literary and Historical Society of Quebec*
HSSM *Transactions of the Historical and Scientific Society of Manitoba*
TRSC *Transactions of the Royal Society of Canada*

PREFACE

1 W.L. Morton ed *The Shield of Achilles: Aspects of Victorian Canada*
 (Toronto 1968) 330

LECTURE ONE: SCIENCE

1 University of Toronto, Thomas Fisher Rare Book Library, Charles Fothergill, ms, 'A Few Notes Made on a Journey from Montreal through the Province of Upper Canada in February, 1817'; J. Baillie 'Charles Fothergill, 1782–1840' *Canadian Historical Review* xxv (Dec 1944) 376–97

2 Major-General Campbell-Hardy 'Reminiscences of a Nova Scotian Naturalist: Andrew Downs' *NSINS* (1906–7) xi–xxix; Harry Piers 'Sketch of the Life of Andrew Downs' ibid (1901–2) cii–cviii

3 R.A. Jarrell 'The Rise and Fall of Science at Quebec' *Histoire Sociale / Social History* x (mai-May 1977) 77–91; Major J. Lachlan *A Retrospective Glance at the Progressive State of the Natural History Society of Montreal* (Montreal 1852)

4 The place of natural history in Victorian Britain is discussed in David E. Allen *The Naturalist in Britain: A Social History* (London 1976), especially chapter 4, and Lynn Barber *The Heyday of Natural History, 1820–1870* (London 1980) chapters 1–2.

5 The following general remarks on these societies are based on an examination of the major journals mentioned in the list of abbreviations, on the unpublished letterbooks and minutes of the Natural History Society of Montreal, in MU, Blacker Wood Library, on the minutes and scrapbooks of the Ottawa Field Naturalists' Club, in PAC, and on the minutes of the Nova Scotian Institute of Natural Science, in PANS, and on secondary studies: W.S. Wallace ed *The Royal Canadian Institute Centennial Volume, 1849–1949* (Toronto 1949), C.B. Fergusson *Nova Scotia Institute of Science* Bulletin of the Public Archives of Nova Scotia no. 18 (Halifax 1963), G.F. Matthew *Sketch of the Natural History Society of New Brunswick* (Saint John 1912), Reverend W.A. Burman 'The Present Status of Natural Science in Manitoba and the Northwest' *HSSM* no. 55 (14 July 1900), Peter Bowler 'The Early Development of Scientific Societies in Canada,' in A. Oleson and S.C. Brown ed *The Pursuit of Knowledge in the Early American Republic* (Baltimore 1976) 326–39, and W.W. Judd *Early Naturalists and Natural History Societies in London, Ontario* (London 1979).

6 John Langton 'Address ...' *LHSQ* ns I (Quebec 1863) 6

7 PANS, Minutes of the Nova Scotian Institute of Natural Science, vol II, 18 Nov 1895

8 M. Zaslow *Reading the Rocks. The Story of the Geological Survey of Canada, 1842–1972* (Ottawa 1975) chapter 6; G.M. Dawson 'On Some of the Larger Unexplored Regions of Canada' *ON* (1890–1) 11

9 Minutes of the Nova Scotia Institute of Natural Science, 6 July 1865

10 Vittorio M.G. De Vecchi *Science and Government in Nineteenth-Century Canada* University of Toronto, PhD thesis, 1978, 40

11 Ann M. Moyal *Scientists in Nineteenth Century Australia: A Documentary History* (Melbourne 1976) 110

12 PAC, Archibald Lampman Papers, Lampman to E.W. Thomson, 6 June 1894

13 MU, J.W. Dawson Papers, Wilson to Dawson, 8 Dec 1881 and 12 Jan 1882

14 Ibid, Dawson to Lorne, 2 Jan 1882 (copy)

15 NC III (déc 1870) 5

16 Ibid I (mai 1869) 142

17 *CNG* II (Nov 1857) 356

18 Bowler 'Early Development' 332. This figure is highly inflated because of the number of Canadians – including politicians and civic boosters – who joined at the time of the Montreal meeting in 1857. By 1860 the American association had only ten Canadian members who took their duties seriously enough to have given one or more papers or who had served on one or more committees; Sally Kohlstedt *The Formation of the American Scientific Community: The American Association for the Advancement of Science, 1848–60* (Urbana, Ill, 1976) 204.

19 The increasing contacts between individual Canadian naturalists and Americans has been abundantly documented. For Dawson see Susan Sheets-Pyenson 'The Formative Years of Canadian Science: John William Dawson and His Circle, 1865–1886' paper presented to the History of Science Society, New York, 30 Dec 1979; for Louis-Ovide Brunet, J.-C.-K. Laflamme, and Provancher, see

Raymond Duchesne 'Science et société coloniale: les natura-
listes du Canada français et leurs correspondants scientifiques
(1860–1900)' *HSTC Bulletin. Journal of the History of Canadian
Science, Technology and Medicine* V (May 1981) 99–139.

20 'Science in Rupert's Land' *CJ* ns VII (1863) 336–47; PAC, Robert
Bell Papers, vol I, Baird to Roderick MacFarlane, 12 April 1865
and 23 Oct 1865; W.H. Dall *Spencer Fullerton Baird* (Philadelphia
1915) 335

21 National Museums of Canada, Macoun Letterbooks, Macoun to
Rhodes, 29 Oct 1893; Macoun to Oldfield Thomas, 26 Nov 1889

22 Ibid, Macoun to Dickson, 16 Feb 1897

23 Ibid, Macoun to George N. Best, 8 Jan 1891

24 W. Waiser 'The Macoun-Merriam Correspondence: Can/Am Natural Science in the Late 19th Century' paper read at the History
of Science Conference, Toronto, October 1980

LECTURE TWO: GOD

1 On the place of natural theology in Canadian philosophy in the
Victorian age, see A.B. McKillop *A Disciplined Intelligence: Critical
Enquiry and Canadian Thought in the Victorian Era* (Montreal 1979)
chapter 4. For a lucid treatment of the American scientific profes-
sion and the uses of religion see George H. Daniels *American
Science in the Age of Jackson* (New York 1968) 49ff.

2 John Keast Lord *The Naturalist on Vancouver Island and British
Columbia* I (London 1866) 345

3 Clarence Glacken *Traces on the Rhodian Shore: Nature and Culture
in Western Thought from Ancient Times to the End of the Eighteenth
Century* (Berkeley 1976) 423; Donald Worster *Nature's Economy:
The Roots of Ecology* (New York 1979) 7

4 Edmund Gosse *The Life of Philip Henry Gosse* (London 1890)
70–1, 75

5 Philip Henry Gosse *The Canadian Naturalist* (London 1840) 337,
360

6 Maria Morris *Wild Flowers of Nova Scotia* (Halifax 1840); Mary
Sparling '"The Lighter Auxiliaries": Women Artists in Nova

Scotia in the Early Nineteenth Century' *Atlantis* V (fall 1979) 99–104

7 Clara Thomas 'Journeys to Freedom' *Canadian Literature* no. 51 (winter 1972) 19; Sara Eaton *Lady of the Backwoods. A Biography of Catherine Parr Traill* (Toronto 1969); E. McCallum 'Catherine Parr Traill: A Nineteenth-Century Ontario Naturalist' *The Beaver* (autumn 1975) 39–45

8 PAC, Traill Family Papers, vol I, James Fletcher to Traill, 21 March 1894. John Macoun was more sceptical, saying she 'was not a critical botanist'; National Museums of Canada, Macoun Letterbook, 1884–8, Macoun to G. Waghorne, 2 Oct 1887.

9 Catherine Parr Traill *Studies of Plant Life in Canada* (Ottawa 1885) 32, 51, 77, 254; 'Flowers and Their Moral Teaching' *BA* I (May 1863) 55–9; Traill Family Papers, Journal 1822–1875, 2987

10 Martin J.S. Rudwick *The Meaning of Fossils: Episodes in the History of Palaeontology* (London 1972) 156–79

11 Charles Coulston Gillespie *Genesis and Geology* (New York 1959) chapter 4; for representative Canadian opinions on his importance see *CNG* II (Mar 1857) 66 and ibid (May 1857) 87. Miller's books, like those of Paley, were prominent in Christian libraries – see *Catalogue of Books and By-Laws of the Mechanics' Institute and Athenaeum, Ottawa* (Ottawa 1867) and *Catalogue of Books in the Library of the Halifax Young Men's Christian Association* (Halifax 1858).

12 Dawson's posthumously published autobiography, *Fifty Years of Work in Canada* (London 1901), offers illuminating illustrations of this way of looking at his own life; so does the self-portrait that his father wrote – see Marjory Whitelaw 'Recollections of His Life, by James Dawson' *Dalhousie Review* LIII (autumn 1973) 501–19.

13 This was invariably the point of departure for such discussions. See Moses Harvey *Lectures on the Harmony of Science and Revelation* (Halifax 1856) and PAC ms, Professor William Kingston 'The Pre-Adamite Age of the Earth, Lecture delivered before the Mechanics' Institute, Cobourg, March 28, 1859.'

14 Dawson *The Testimony of the Holy Scriptures Respecting Wine and Strong Drink ...* (Pictou, NS, 1858), originally published in 1848.

For a more detailed treatment see Charles F. O'Brien *Sir William Dawson: A Life in Science and Religion* (Philadelphia 1971) chapter 3.

15 'Catalogue of a few remarkable coincidences, etc., which induce a belief of the Asiatic origin of the North American Indians, by Major Mercer' *LHSQ* (Quebec 1829) 241–2

16 Captain J.H. Lefroy 'On the Probable Number of the Native Population of British America' *CJ* I (April 1853) 193; see also 'Annual Report of the Council' ibid VII (Mar 1857) 148.

17 William Stanton *The Leopard's Spots: Scientific Attitudes Toward Race in America, 1815–1859* (Chicago 1966) 192

18 *Archaia* (Montreal 1860) 246

19 Reverend William McLaren *The Unity of the Human Race. A Lecture delivered before the members of the Belleville Young Men's Christian Association on the evening of the 19th March, 1860* (Belleville 1860); see also *Annual Address, Delivered by Professor Jack, A.M., President, before the Fredericton Athenaeum, February 20, 1854* (Fredericton 1854) 11–14.

20 MU Archives, Dawson Papers, Scrapbook, 'Old Letters,' Wilson to Dawson, 12 July 1857. Wilson's paper is summarized in *CNG* II (Sept 1857) 289–91 and the argument elaborated in 'Illustrative Examples of Some Modifying Elements Affecting the Ethnic Significance of Peculiar Forms of the Human Skull' *CJ* VI (1861) 414–25 and 'Ethnical Forms and Undesigned Artificial Distortions of the Human Cranium' ibid VII (Sept 1862) 399–446. On Wilson and Dawson as anthropologists see Bruce Trigger 'Sir Daniel Wilson: Canada's First Anthropologist' and 'Sir William Dawson: A Faithful Anthropologist' *Anthropologica* VII (1966) 3–37, 351–8. Wilson's work has been set into the context of the history of the discipline in D. Cole 'The Origins of Canadian Anthropology, 1850–1910' *Journal of Canadian Studies* VIII (Feb 1973) 33–45 and Bennett McCardle *The Life and Anthropological Works of Daniel Wilson, 1816–1892* University of Toronto, MA thesis, 1980.

21 Wilson 'Brain-Weight and Size in Relation to Relative Capacity of Races' *CJ* XV (Oct 1876) 180

22 R.G. Haliburton 'The Festival of the Dead' *NSINS* I (1863) 61–85;
William Gossip 'The Affinity of Races' ibid III part III (1873) 288–315

23 James Bovell *Outlines of Natural Theology for the Use of the Canadian Student* (Toronto 1859), which is discussed in C.E. Dolman 'The Reverend James Bovell, M.D., 1817–1880' in G.F.G. Stanley ed *Pioneers of Canadian Science* (Toronto 1966) 81–100 and McKillop *A Disciplined Intelligence* 73–85

24 Bethune 'Insect Life in Canada – March and April' *BA* I (May 1863) 85

25 *Archaia* 356

26 *CNG* VII (Feb 1863) 68

27 'Glaucus, or the Wonders of the Shore' *CNG* I (Jan 1857) 464; Couper 'The Orders, Sub-Orders and Genera of Insects' *TLHSQ* session 1863–4 ns (Quebec 1864) 158; PAC, Bell Papers, vol XXXVII, ms, 'Address to the Convocation of Queen's University, Kingston, 25 April 1883' 5

28 James Barnston 'General Remarks on the Study of Nature ...' *CNG* II (Mar 1857) 39–40; Macoun Letterbook, 1884–1888, Macoun to N.S. Bebb, 5 Oct 1887

29 David E. Allen *The Naturalist in Britain* (London 1976) 76

30 Philip Carteret Hill *Unity in Creation: A Lecture Delivered before the Halifax Young Men's Christian Association, February 3, 1857* (Halifax 1857)

31 A. Macallum *Synopsis of Natural History* (Toronto 1857)

32 Joseph Howe *An Opening Address, Delivered at the first meeting of the Halifax Mechanics' Institute, on Wednesday, January 11, 1832* (Halifax 1832) 4; PAC, John Sparrow Thompson Papers, vol V, 'Halifax Mechanics' Institute Letter Book, 1832–1830,' George R. Young, 'Science,' May 1835. On the social implications of geology in the first half of the century, see Gillespie *Genesis and Geology* chapter 7.

LECTURE THREE: NATURE

1 MU Archives, Dawson Papers, Box 21, Lyell to Dawson, 27 Oct 1860

2 James R. Moore *The Post-Darwinian Controversies; A Study of the Protestant Struggle to Come to Terms with Darwin in Great Britain and America, 1870–1900* (Cambridge 1979) 92

3 Peter J. Vorzimmer *Charles Darwin: The Years of Controversy: The Origin of Species and Its Critics, 1859–1882* (Philadelphia 1970)

4 Alvar Ellegard *Darwin and the General Reader: The Reception of Darwin's Theory of Evolution in the British Periodical Press, 1859–1872* (Göteborg 1958) 132

5 Dawson *CNG* V (Feb 1860) 100–20; Wilson *CJ* V (Mar 1860) 116–21 and VI (Mar 1861) 113–19; Chapman *CJ* V (1860) 367–87. For accounts of the reception of Darwin in the Canadian intellectual community see Charles F. O'Brien *Sir William Dawson* (Philadelphia 1971) chapter 5; A.B. McKillop *A Disciplined Intelligence* (Montreal 1979) chapter 4; Robert Taylor *The Darwinian Revolution: The Responses of Four Canadian Scholars* McMaster University, Ph D thesis, 1976; P. Roome 'The Darwin Debate in Canada: 1860–1880' in L.A. Knafla et al ed *Science, Technology, and Culture in Historical Perspective* (Calgary 1972) 183–99; and Howard V. Reimer *Darwinism in Canadian Literature* McMaster University, Ph D thesis, 1975, which is concerned with an imaginative continuum in literature.

6 Martin J.S. Rudwick *The Meaning of Fossils: Episodes in the History of Palaeontology* (London 1972) 236

7 These patterns were traced in all of Dawson's popular works, but most comprehensively in *The Chain of Life in Geological Time: A Sketch of the Origin and Succession of Animals and Plants* (London 1895).

8 William Hincks *CJ* VIII (Sept 1863) 397

9 Dawson 'Modern Ideas of Derivation' *CN* ns IV (June 1869) 137–8

10 Neal C. Gillespie *Charles Darwin and the Problem of Creation* (Chicago 1979) 21–2

11 *CJ* V (1860) 386

12 Dawson 'Annual Address' *CN* VII (1875) 290 and *Some Salient Points in the History of the Earth* (New York 1894) 191

13 Moore *Post-Darwinian Controversies* 204, 214

14 Dawson *Some Salient Points* 117; for an early attempt based on this passage to make Dawson out to be a more accommodating critic see J.C. Sutherland 'Sir William Dawson and Evolution' *Queen's Quarterly* XVII (Jan 1910) 212–17.

15 Dawson *The Story of the Earth and Man* 8th edn (London 1883) 396

16 Charles Gillispie *Genesis and Geology* (New York 1959) 227

17 Dawson Papers, Box 4, C.G. Stokes to Dawson, 21 Mar 1871; Michael Ruse *The Darwinian Revolution* (Chicago 1978) 259–60

18 Dawson Papers, Box 6, Dawson to Royal Society, 7 Dec 1877 (draft); J.J. Bigsby to Dawson, 21 Jan 1878

19 Dawson *The Story* 312

20 Dawson Papers, Box 6, Dawson to Charles Hodge, 15 Apr 1878

21 Raymond Duchesne 'La Bibliothèque scientifique de l'abbé Léon Provancher' *Revue d'histoire de l'Amérique française* XXXIV (mars 1981) 535–6

22 Daniel Wilson *Caliban: the Missing Link* (London 1873) 190

23 Daniel Wilson *Address at the Convocation of University College, Toronto, October 16, 1885* (Toronto 1885) 11

24 University of Toronto Archives, Fisher Library, Daniel Wilson Diary, 7 and 28 Mar 1887; *The Week* (17 Mar 1887) 263–4

25 Dawson Papers, Wilson to Dawson, 9 Feb 1888

26 PAC, Robert Bell Papers, vol XXXVI, ms, 'Personal Reminiscences of Sir William Logan,' 41

27 *Autobiography of John Macoun* (Ottawa 1922) 39

28 Joseph W. Bailey *Loring Woart Bailey: The Story of a Man of Science* (Saint John 1925) 65–6

29 *BA* I (June 1863) 203–4; PAC, Traill Family Papers, vol I, Fletcher to Traill, 28 Mar 1883

30 MU, Blacker Wood Library, Natural History Society of Montreal Minute Book, Mar 1830; MU Archives, Sir William Logan papers, W.S. Goldie to Logan, 14 Mar 1856; Thomas C. Weston *Reminiscences among the Rocks in Connection with the Geological Survey of Canada* (Toronto 1898) 128–9; *The Acadian Scientist* I (Feb 1883) 2

31 A. Leith Adams *Field and Forest Rambles* (London 1873) 191

32 PANS, Nova Scotia Institute of Natural Science, General Minutes, vol I, 1862–77, 7 Mar 1864; Lawson 'Remarks on the Flora of the Northern Shores of America' *TRSC* (1887) 207–12

33 W. Mills *The Nature and Development of Animal Intelligence* (London 1898) 20

34 A.H. Mackay 'Botanical Nomenclature' *The Acadian Scientist* I (Aug 1883); R.R. Wright *An Introduction to Zoology for the Use of Schools* (Toronto 1889) chapter 10, 'General Principles'

35 Robert Campbell 'A Sketch of the Progress of Botany in the Nineteenth Century' *Canadian Record of Science* IX (Jan 1903) 39–53

36 Ann M. Moyal *Scientists in Nineteenth Century Australia: A Documentary History* (Melbourne 1976) 189; E.W. MacBride 'The Present Position of Evolution' *ON* XVI (May 1902) 56–8. For two more qualified assessments by academic naturalists see A.B. Macallum 'The Semi-Centennial of the Origin of Species' *TRSC* (1909) 177–90 and R. Ramsay Wright 'The Progress of Biology' *TRSC* (1912) xxxvii–xlviii

37 Frank Adams 'Sir John William Dawson' *Canadian Record of Science* VIII (Jan 1900) 147; Henry Ami 'Annual Address of the President' *ON* XIII (Feb 1900) 273

38 E.W. MacBride 'Zoological Problems for the Natural History Society of Montreal' *CRS* VIII (Jan 1899) 10

Index